JUMBLE®

Birthday

Perfect Puzzle Presents for Every Person!

Henri Arnold,
Bob Lee,
Mike Argirion,
Jeff Knurek, &
David L. Hoyt

TRIUMPH
BOOKS

For further information, contact:
Triumph Books LLC
814 North Franklin Street
Chicago, Illinois 60610
Phone: (312) 337-0747
www.triumphbooks.com

Printed in U.S.A.
ISBN: 978-1-629-37652-3

Design by Sue Knopf

Contents

JUMBLE®

Birthday

Classic Puzzles

JUMBLE®

Unscramble these four Jumbles, one letter
to each square, to form four ordinary words.

RABIR

SYSUF

HISRAP

LOYDOG

THESE ATHLETES CAN
BE EXPECTED TO START
PROSPERING.

Now arrange the circled letters to form
the surprise answer, as suggested by the
above cartoon.

Print answer here  " ◯◯◯◯ "

2

JUMBLE®

Unscramble these four Jumbles, one letter
to each square, to form four ordinary words.

NERAV

HESER

TUSJAD

MALEYS

WHAT SHE GAVE THE
MOUNTAIN CLIMBER.

Now arrange the circled letters to form
the surprise answer, as suggested by the
above cartoon.

Print answer here ◯◯◯ "◯◯◯◯◯◯"

JUMBLE®

Unscramble these four Jumbles, one letter to each square, to form four ordinary words.

DROAH

ODITI

SIBULY

FLUITE

THEY'RE THREE TO ONE!

Now arrange the circled letters to form the surprise answer, as suggested by the above cartoon.

Print answer here ⬡⬡⬡⬡⬡⬡⬡

JUMBLE®

Unscramble these four Jumbles, one letter
to each square, to form four ordinary words.

PRIGE

RYTUL

ENBOGE

FLAMEE

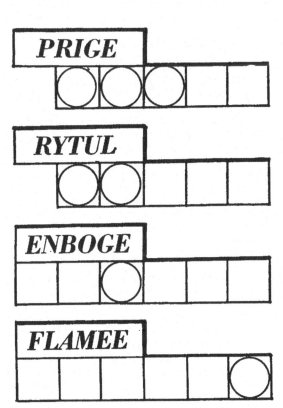

IN CASE OF
FIRE — PULL!

Now arrange the circled letters to form
the surprise answer, as suggested by the
above cartoon.

Print answer here **THE**

5

JUMBLE®

Unscramble these four Jumbles, one letter to each square, to form four ordinary words.

CAFTE

⬜⬜⬜⬜⬜

TAREF

⬜⬜⬜⬜⬜

MOCINE

⬜⬜⬜⬜⬜⬜

TEMNEC

⬜⬜⬜⬜⬜⬜

You back again?

Move on!

COMES AND GOES IN THE STREET.

Now arrange the circled letters to form the surprise answer, as suggested by the above cartoon.

Print answer here ⬜⬜⬜⬜⬜⬜⬜

JUMBLE®

Unscramble these four Jumbles, one letter
to each square, to form four ordinary words.

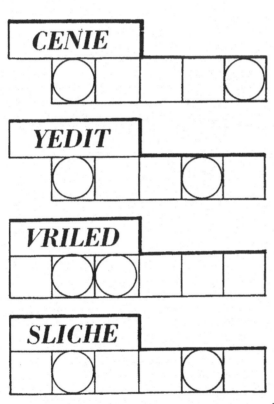

CENIE

YEDIT

VRILED

SLICHE

Put it
on my
tab

But . . . your
credit, sir . . .

COULD BE "IN THE RED"
—BUT HE'S STILL
ABLE TO EATOUT.

Now arrange the circled letters to form
the surprise answer, as suggested by the
above cartoon.

Print answer here

JUMBLE®

Unscramble these four Jumbles, one letter to each square, to form four ordinary words.

VINGY

DRUGO

PHATAY

LENETS

LETTERS CALLING FOR AN ANSWER.

HA! Several invites!

Now arrange the circled letters to form the surprise answer, as suggested by the above cartoon.

Print answer here ⬡⬡⬡⬡

JUMBLE®

Unscramble these four Jumbles, one letter to each square, to form four ordinary words.

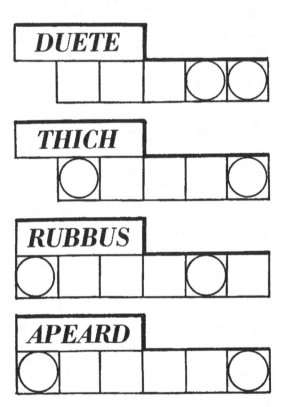

DUETE

THICH

RUBBUS

APEARD

HE MIGHT BE ASSOCIATED WITH A CROOK.

Now arrange the circled letters to form the surprise answer, as suggested by the above cartoon.

Print answer here A

JUMBLE®

Unscramble these four Jumbles, one letter
to each square, to form four ordinary words.

NUGOY

STEAE

BUSTIM

ZOAMAN

AL'S SERVICE STATION

NO CHARGE UNLESS IT'S FIXED

Now arrange the circled letters to form
the surprise answer, as suggested by the
above cartoon.

Print answer here **A**

JUMBLE®

Unscramble these four Jumbles, one letter to each square, to form four ordinary words.

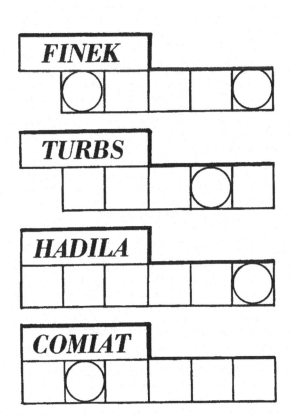

FINEK

TURBS

HADILA

COMIAT

Very rare these days!

FOUR-FIFTHS OF IT IS WOODEN BUT IT STILL TASTES GOOD.

Now arrange the circled letters to form the surprise answer, as suggested by the above cartoon.

Print answer here

11

JUMBLE®

Unscramble these four Jumbles, one letter
to each square, to form four ordinary words.

Cherchez la femme?

NO!

SOUNDS AS THOUGH
THE CRIMINAL WAS
NOT A WOMAN.

DALLE

YAIRF

PREEMT

NOBARC

Now arrange the circled letters to form
the surprise answer, as suggested by the
above cartoon.

Print answer here **THE** " ⬡⬡⬡⬡ - ⬡⬡⬡⬡⬡⬡ "

JUMBLE®

Unscramble these four Jumbles, one letter
to each square, to form four ordinary words.

GLARN

ATEEN

LENOTS

FORPIT

THEY DON'T HAVE TO
BE CIVIL WHEN THEY
DO THEIR WORK.

Now arrange the circled letters to form
the surprise answer, as suggested by the
above cartoon.

Print answer here

JUMBLE®

Unscramble these four Jumbles, one letter
to each square, to form four ordinary words.

ALVAN

NEMIR

POWALL

EMSIDE

SUCH A MAN
IS REALLY OF
LOW DEGREE.

Now arrange the circled letters to form
the surprise answer, as suggested by the
above cartoon.

Print answer here **A**

JUMBLE®

Unscramble these four Jumbles, one letter
to each square, to form four ordinary words.

KECHE

CHAVO

LOCHOS

YAIWAR

Hi, Sweetie!

Hmph!

EVIDENTLY THIS KIND
OF OWL DOESN'T
GIVE A HOOT!

Now arrange the circled letters to form
the surprise answer, as suggested by the
above cartoon.

Print answer here **A** ⬡⬡⬡⬡⬡⬡⬡⬡ ⬡⬡⬡

15

JUMBLE®

Unscramble these four Jumbles, one letter
to each square, to form four ordinary words.

GAGBY

OJYLL

FLOBIE

DRIVEA

EGG PRODUCTION

1973   1974

THE SHAPE OF THINGS
TO COME IN THE
POULTRY BUSINESS.

Now arrange the circled letters to form
the surprise answer, as suggested by the
above cartoon.

Print answer here

JUMBLE®

Unscramble these four Jumbles, one letter to each square, to form four ordinary words.

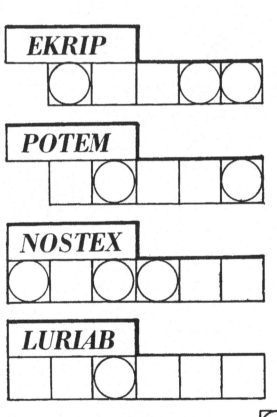

EKRIP

POTEM

NOSTEX

LURIAB

Immediate delivery

BILL OF SALE

THEIR EFFORTS BRING CREDIT TO THEIR COUNTRY.

Now arrange the circled letters to form the surprise answer, as suggested by the above cartoon.

Print answer here

17

JUMBLE®

Unscramble these four Jumbles, one letter
to each square, to form four ordinary words.

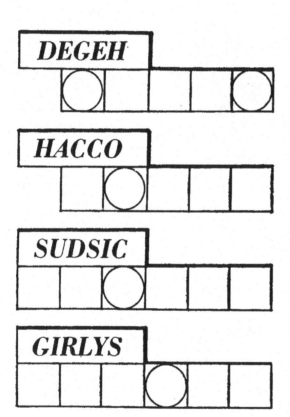

DEGEH

HACCO

SUDSIC

GIRLYS

My bill will help citizens like yourself.

DESIGNED TO SUPPORT THE MEMBERS AT THE BOTTOM.

Now arrange the circled letters to form
the surprise answer, as suggested by the
above cartoon.

Print answer here ⬡⬡⬡⬡⬡

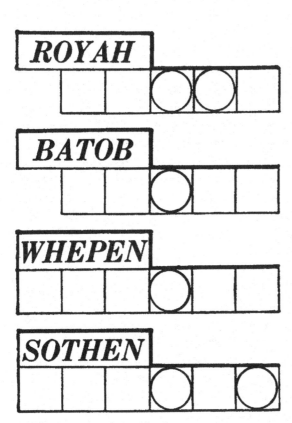

JUMBLE®

Unscramble these four Jumbles, one letter to each square, to form four ordinary words.

ROYAH

BATOB

WHEPEN

SOTHEN

Your first social security check!

HAPPY RETIREMENT

YOU CAN DRAW THIS AS LONG AS YOU LIVE.

Now arrange the circled letters to form the surprise answer, as suggested by the above cartoon.

Print answer here

JUMBLE®

Unscramble these four Jumbles, one letter
to each square, to form four ordinary words.

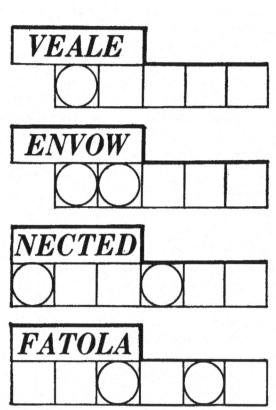

VEALE

ENVOW

NECTED

FATOLA

I don't mind, dear

NOTHING PAID YET—
AND NO OBJECTIONS!

Now arrange the circled letters to form
the surprise answer, as suggested by the
above cartoon.

Print answer here "◯◯◯ – ◯◯◯◯"

20

JUMBLE

Unscramble these four Jumbles, one letter
to each square, to form four ordinary words.

FECEN

LAASI

BLAMME

GLEZUZ

Your dinner, dear

Dad, help me
with my
arithmetic

A SIGN THAT
ONE'S REDUCING.

Now arrange the circled letters to form
the surprise answer, as suggested by the
above cartoon.

Print answer here

JUMBLE®

Unscramble these four Jumbles, one letter
to each square, to form four ordinary words.

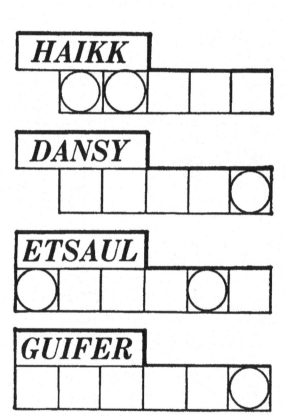

HAIKK

DANSY

ETSAUL

GUIFER

What a beautiful morning

WHEN BLUE THINGS
MIGHT LOOK BRIGHTER.

Now arrange the circled letters to form
the surprise answer, as suggested by the
above cartoon.

Print answer here

22

JUMBLE

Unscramble these four Jumbles, one letter to each square, to form four ordinary words.

CLUHG

WELJE

NAIGAN

HONGIM

THAT "BULL" ACROSS THE ATLANTIC.

Now arrange the circled letters to form the surprise answer, as suggested by the above cartoon.

Print answer here " ◯◯◯◯ "

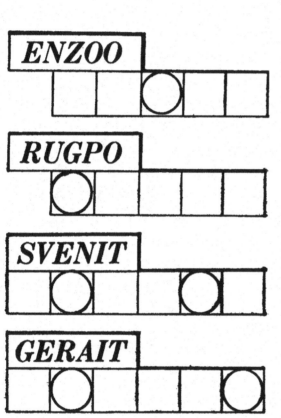

JUMBLE®

Unscramble these four Jumbles, one letter
to each square, to form four ordinary words.

ENZOO

RUGPO

SVENIT

GERAIT

Tsk! Need a
new one!

**WHAT ORGANS
MIGHT ALSO PRODUCE.**

Now arrange the circled letters to form
the surprise answer, as suggested by the
above cartoon.

Print answer here

JUMBLE®

Unscramble these four Jumbles, one letter
to each square, to form four ordinary words.

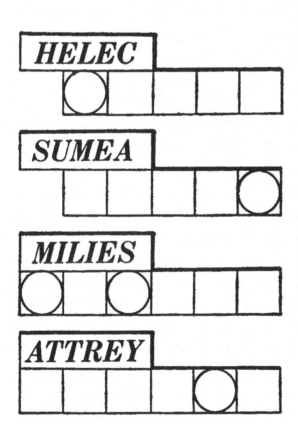

HELEC

SUMEA

MILIES

ATTREY

SELLING
OUT
LOST OUR
LEASE

GOES INTO
LIQUIDATION WHEN
THE HEAT'S ON.

Now arrange the circled letters to form
the surprise answer, as suggested by the
above cartoon.

Print answer here

JUMBLE®

Unscramble these four Jumbles, one letter
to each square, to form four ordinary words.

PENIT

TOANB

SENFUI

DABBIE

MATERNITY

He's
nuts!

SOUNDS CRAZY
ABOUT BASEBALL.

Now arrange the circled letters to form
the surprise answer, as suggested by the
above cartoon.

Print answer here " ⬡⬡⬡⬡ "

26

JUMBLE®
Birthday

Daily
Puzzles

JUMBLE®

Unscramble these four Jumbles, one letter
to each square, to form four ordinary words.

YADDD

LARNS

GLEIMN

ZURQAT

TREE OF KNOWLEDGE

my
mine
our
ours

FIRST PERSON POSSESSIVE.

Now arrange the circled letters to form
the surprise answer, as suggested by the
above cartoon.

Print answer here ◯◯◯◯◯'◯

28

JUMBLE®

Unscramble these four Jumbles, one letter to each square, to form four ordinary words.

NADAP

YUTIN

BLATUR

REOCAN

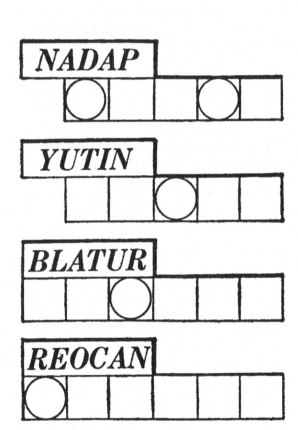

CARDIAC WARD

Guess he's cured

THE MOST FAMOUS HEART SPECIALIST.

Now arrange the circled letters to form the surprise answer, as suggested by the above cartoon.

Print answer here

JUMBLE®

Unscramble these four Jumbles, one letter
to each square, to form four ordinary words.

Makes me sick
to my stomach

OUR
LEADER

SUFFERERS FROM
THIS AGREE IT
COULD BE CRUEL.

ELLIB

URRYC

SLYJUT

UMSOUC

Now arrange the circled letters to form
the surprise answer, as suggested by the
above cartoon.

Print answer here

JUMBLE®

Unscramble these four Jumbles, one letter
to each square, to form four ordinary words.

VELOH

DAMEF

LIZZES

TENAGE

Contemptible!

HIS SOLE
COMPANION.

Now arrange the circled letters to form
the surprise answer, as suggested by the
above cartoon.

Print answer here

JUMBLE®

Unscramble these four Jumbles, one letter to each square, to form four ordinary words.

THACC

⬚ ◯ ⬚ ⬚ ⬚

RUCOS

◯ ⬚ ⬚ ⬚ ⬚

GINOUT

⬚ ⬚ ⬚ ⬚ ◯ ⬚

MERPIT

◯ ⬚ ⬚ ⬚ ⬚ ⬚

BORDER

"I GET OUT OF SPAIN — GOING ACROSS A RIVER!"

Now arrange the circled letters to form the surprise answer, as suggested by the above cartoon.

Print answer here " ◯ ◯ ◯ ◯ "

JUMBLE.

Unscramble these four Jumbles, one letter
to each square, to form four ordinary words.

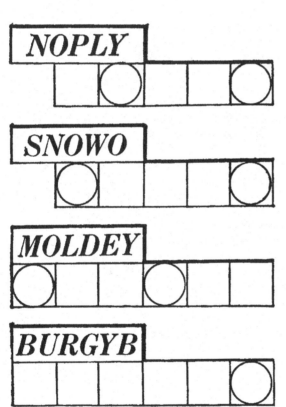

NOPLY

SNOWO

MOLDEY

BURGYB

What's it mean?

Check the dictionary

IN A WORD, IT MEANS THE SAME THING!

Now arrange the circled letters to form
the surprise answer, as suggested by the
above cartoon.

Print answer here

JUMBLE®

Unscramble these four Jumbles, one letter
to each square, to form four ordinary words.

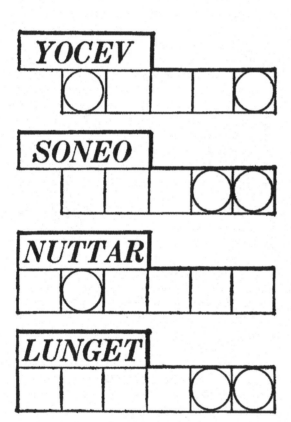

YOCEV

SONEO

NUTTAR

LUNGET

How much
will you
need?

ACT ONE

MIGHT PROVIDE
BACKING FOR A PLAY.

Now arrange the circled letters to form
the surprise answer, as suggested by the
above cartoon.

Print answer here

JUMBLE®

Unscramble these four Jumbles, one letter
to each square, to form four ordinary words.

LIPUP

BICCU

TOWBES

SLUDOH

Wears like
iron

Got her
trained

THE CAVEMAN'S
STRONGEST SUIT.

Now arrange the circled letters to form
the surprise answer, as suggested by the
above cartoon.

Print answer here

35

JUMBLE®

Unscramble these four Jumbles, one letter
to each square, to form four ordinary words.

MARRO

TISPE

ETOGEA

DAHNED

Darn! I made
a mistake!

RUB AWAY!

Now arrange the circled letters to form
the surprise answer, as suggested by the
above cartoon.

Print answer here " ◯◯◯◯◯ "

JUMBLE

Unscramble these four Jumbles, one letter
to each square, to form four ordinary words.

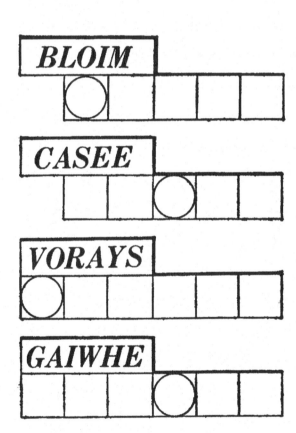

BLOIM

CASEE

VORAYS

GAIWHE

FEELS SICK—
FROM A SAIL.

Now arrange the circled letters to form
the surprise answer, as suggested by the
above cartoon.

Print answer here

37

JUMBLE®

Unscramble these four Jumbles, one letter
to each square, to form four ordinary words.

AGREW

WALBY

PLECOM

SHOOTE

WHAT A LIFE ON THE
OCEAN WAVE IS.

Now arrange the circled letters to form
the surprise answer, as suggested by the
above cartoon.

Print answer here " ⬡⬡⬡⬡⬡ "

JUMBLE®

Unscramble these four Jumbles, one letter to each square, to form four ordinary words.

ATLAN

LORBI

TRAPCE

DAZIOC

A FORMER LEADING LADY IN RUSSIA.

Now arrange the circled letters to form the surprise answer, as suggested by the above cartoon.

Print answer here

JUMBLE®

Unscramble these four Jumbles, one letter to each square, to form four ordinary words.

ICHED

YURUS

SEECIX

ROLMAN

I'm here for the trash

MAY BE TAKEN FROM HOME WITH PLEASURE.

Now arrange the circled letters to form the surprise answer, as suggested by the above cartoon.

Print answer here **AN** ⬡⬡⬡⬡⬡⬡⬡⬡⬡⬡

JUMBLE®

Unscramble these four Jumbles, one letter
to each square, to form four ordinary words.

NORIB

CADYE

REENOC

ZANATS

From the butcher.
Guess how much?

A NOTABLE
INCREASE.

Now arrange the circled letters to form
the surprise answer, as suggested by the
above cartoon.

Print answer here

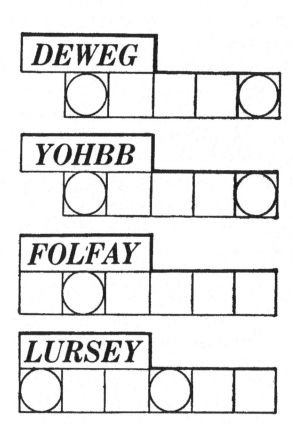

JUMBLE®

Unscramble these four Jumbles, one letter to each square, to form four ordinary words.

DEWEG

YOHBB

FOLFAY

LURSEY

See? A sound investment!

GOLD STOCK IN PATAGONIA

THIS LIQUID MIGHT BE DECEIVING.

Now arrange the circled letters to form the surprise answer, as suggested by the above cartoon.

Print answer here

JUMBLE®

Unscramble these four Jumbles, one letter
to each square, to form four ordinary words.

KALEY

CELER

DENGER

GROFTE

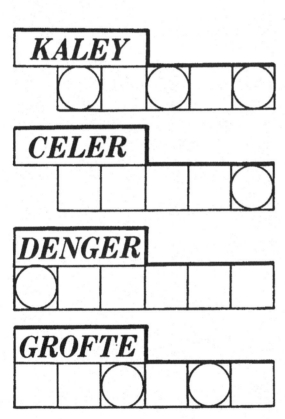

Achoo!

Gesundheit!

WHAT YOU MIGHT FIND
IN THE GALLERY.

Now arrange the circled letters to form
the surprise answer, as suggested by the
above cartoon.

Print answer here "〇〇〇〇〇〇〇"

43

JUMBLE®

Unscramble these four Jumbles, one letter
to each square, to form four ordinary words.

CHIRB

VEROL

BABFLY

FADGYL

Did you start that fire?

ASK A BURNING
QUESTION.

Now arrange the circled letters to form
the surprise answer, as suggested by the
above cartoon.

Print answer here ⬭⬭⬭⬭⬭

44

JUMBLE®

Unscramble these four Jumbles, one letter to each square, to form four ordinary words.

REDON

DUGEF

FINTEC

WETING

Some-
one
goofed!

WHAT YOU WOULDN'T
HAVE A SINGLE
REASON FOR GETTING.

Now arrange the circled letters to form the surprise answer, as suggested by the above cartoon.

Print answer here **A**

JUMBLE®

Unscramble these four Jumbles, one letter to each square, to form four ordinary words.

YEASS

ABOOT

NIFTIE

CAMEEN

WHERE LOGS AREN'T FOR BURNING.

Now arrange the circled letters to form the surprise answer, as suggested by the above cartoon.

Print answer here

JUMBLE

Unscramble these four Jumbles, one letter
to each square, to form four ordinary words.

GYTIN

RASCY

SUREDS

LAFTES

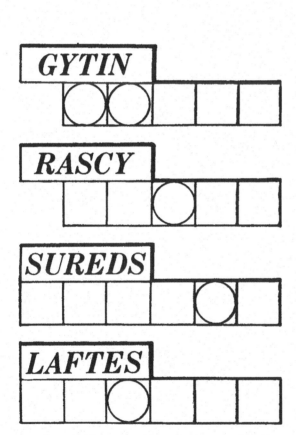

I'm not leaving after all!

REMAINS — TO
PROVIDE SUPPORT.

Now arrange the circled letters to form
the surprise answer, as suggested by the
above cartoon.

Print answer here

47

JUMBLE®

Unscramble these four Jumbles, one letter to each square, to form four ordinary words.

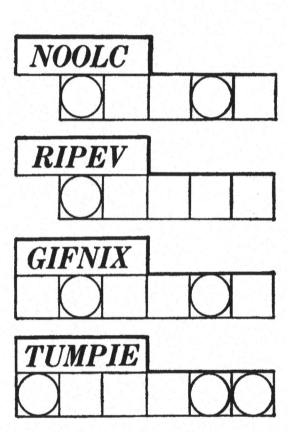

NOOLC

RIPEV

GIFNIX

TUMPIE

MAKES YOU FEEL PUT OUT.

Now arrange the circled letters to form the surprise answer, as suggested by the above cartoon.

Print answer here **AN** ⬚⬚⬚⬚⬚⬚⬚⬚

JUMBLE®

Unscramble these four Jumbles, one letter
to each square, to form four ordinary words.

CLOIG

ZEBAL

INCUVA

DANCEN

SWEET ADELINE

Sick
friend . .

WHAT THE STONE
AGE MAN DID WHEN
HE CAME HOME
LATE ONE NIGHT.

Now arrange the circled letters to form
the surprise answer, as suggested by the
above cartoon.

Print answer here

49

JUMBLE®

Unscramble these four Jumbles, one letter
to each square, to form four ordinary words.

KYMIL

TRAAL

MODCEY

SLAVNY

WHAT THAT AWFUL
SINGER WAS.

Now arrange the circled letters to form
the surprise answer, as suggested by the
above cartoon.

Print answer here A " ◯◯◯◯◯ – ◯◯◯◯◯ "

JUMBLE®

Unscramble these four Jumbles, one letter
to each square, to form four ordinary words.

THABE

ECTAN

SKROHE

CEADAR

It's in very quiet
good taste

WHAT A TASTEFUL
NECKTIE SHOULD BE.

Now arrange the circled letters to form
the surprise answer, as suggested by the
above cartoon.

Print
answer
here

BUT
NOT

" "

JUMBLE®

Unscramble these four Jumbles, one letter
to each square, to form four ordinary words.

KIHCC

FYFAT

TICCAR

LARBUT

WHAT DERMATOLOGY
IS THE SCIENCE OF.

Now arrange the circled letters to form
the surprise answer, as suggested by the
above cartoon.

Print answer here " ⃝⃝⃝⃝ ⃝⃝⃝⃝⃝ "

JUMBLE®

Unscramble these four Jumbles, one letter
to each square, to form four ordinary words.

RUPEN

ORNED

MESTIK

LAFTUR

Tell me more

WHAT A FLATTERER
SELDOM IS.

Now arrange the circled letters to form
the surprise answer, as suggested by the
above cartoon.

Print answer here

53

JUMBLE®

Unscramble these four Jumbles, one letter
to each square, to form four ordinary words.

BELLI

VALIE

VORAYS

DULCOY

HOW THAT
COMICAL SERGEANT
STARTED THE DAY
FOR HIS TROOPS.

Now arrange the circled letters to form
the surprise answer, as suggested by the
above cartoon.

Print answer here WITH " ⬡⬡⬡⬡⬡ " ⬡⬡⬡⬡

JUMBLE®

Unscramble these four Jumbles, one letter to each square, to form four ordinary words.

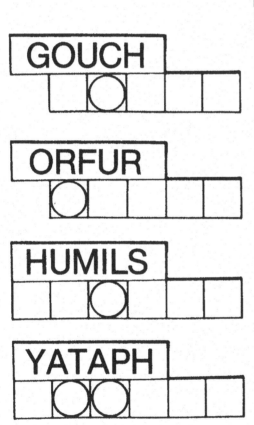

GOUCH

ORFUR

HUMILS

YATAPH

He's stealing the show

Until now I was falling asleep

WHAT THE ACROBAT MADE A SUCCESS OF.

Now arrange the circled letters to form the surprise answer, as suggested by the above cartoon.

Print answer here ☐ " ☐☐☐☐ "

JUMBLE®

Unscramble these four Jumbles, one letter
to each square, to form four ordinary words.

BISSA

PEECA

TURAIN

BOAMEA

WHAT THE POOREST
WAITERS IN SOME
RESTAURANTS ARE.

Now arrange the circled letters to form
the surprise answer, as suggested by the
above cartoon.

Print answer here

JUMBLE®

Unscramble these four Jumbles, one letter
to each square, to form four ordinary words.

OINES

SOULY

SHUBAM

DUSHOL

WAS THE CLAM
DIGGER THIS?

Now arrange the circled letters to form
the surprise answer, as suggested by the
above cartoon.

Print
answer
here

"◯◯◯◯◯◯" ◯◯◯◯◯

JUMBLE®

Unscramble these four Jumbles, one letter
to each square, to form four ordinary words.

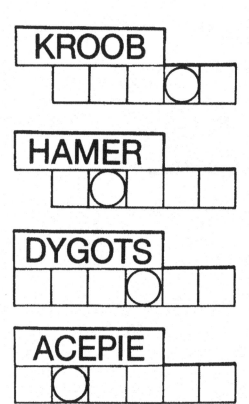

KROOB

HAMER

DYGOTS

ACEPIE

We grow all our
own vegetables

FULL OF BEANS!

Now arrange the circled letters to form
the surprise answer, as suggested by the
above cartoon.

Print answer here

JUMBLE®

Unscramble these four Jumbles, one letter
to each square, to form four ordinary words.

SUMIC

TEABA

ASTOAN

MOYPLE

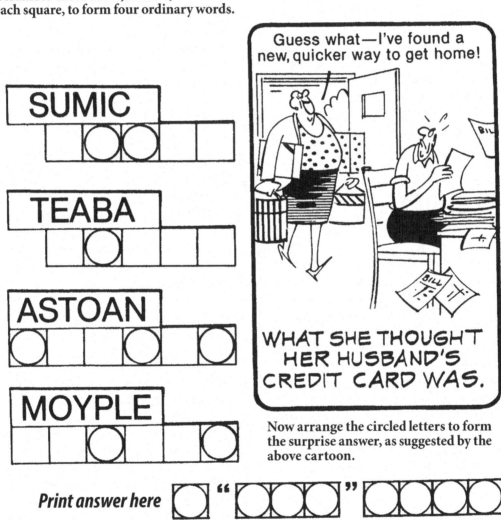

Guess what—I've found a new, quicker way to get home!

WHAT SHE THOUGHT HER HUSBAND'S CREDIT CARD WAS.

Now arrange the circled letters to form
the surprise answer, as suggested by the
above cartoon.

Print answer here ◯ " ◯◯◯ " ◯◯◯◯

JUMBLE®

Unscramble these four Jumbles, one letter to each square, to form four ordinary words.

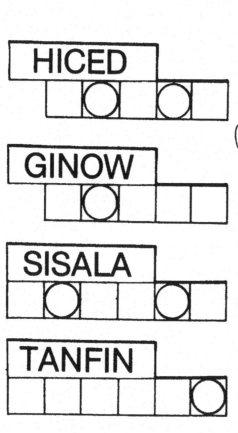

HICED

GINOW

SISALA

TANFIN

I could eat a horse!

Oh, no you don't!

HEALTH FOOD BAR

PEOPLE GO TO GREAT "LENGTHS" TO REDUCE THIS.

Now arrange the circled letters to form the surprise answer, as suggested by the above cartoon.

Print answer here

JUMBLE®

Unscramble these four Jumbles, one letter to each square, to form four ordinary words.

LAIDY

MOBUX

REESIO

BENTON

WHAT PEOPLE WITH TIRELESS ENERGY OFTEN BECOME.

Now arrange the circled letters to form the surprise answer, as suggested by the above cartoon.

Print answer here ◯◯◯◯◯◯◯◯◯

JUMBLE®

Unscramble these four Jumbles, one letter
to each square, to form four ordinary words.

CLUNE

MALUB

DEBIHN

UFTOIT

WHAT THAT
GORGEOUS
SKY WAS.

Now arrange the circled letters to form
the surprise answer, as suggested by the
above cartoon.

Print answer here "◯◯◯◯ – ◯◯◯◯◯"

JUMBLE®

Unscramble these four Jumbles, one letter
to each square, to form four ordinary words.

GNUST

SHYKU

BUNNIO

YANTID

WHEN THE FAMOUS
STAR DIDN'T SHOW
UP, HIS STAND-IN
BECAME THIS.

Now arrange the circled letters to form
the surprise answer, as suggested by the
above cartoon.

Print answer here A ⭕⭕⭕⭕⭕⭕⭕⭕⭕

JUMBLE®

Unscramble these four Jumbles, one letter
to each square, to form four ordinary words.

REEMY

DESET

WILDEM

TRUIPY

WHAT A BELLY
DANCER HAS TO
KNOW HOW TO DO.

Now arrange the circled letters to form
the surprise answer, as suggested by the
above cartoon.

Print
answer
here

⬡⬡⬡⬡⬡⬡⬡ HER " ⬡⬡⬡ "

JUMBLE®

Unscramble these four Jumbles, one letter
to each square, to form four ordinary words.

RYCED

WEJEL

INGADE

NAULCY

THAT HAMMY
MAGICIAN KNEW HOW
TO MAKE THIS
DISAPPEAR.

Now arrange the circled letters to form
the surprise answer, as suggested by the
above cartoon.

Print answer here THE

JUMBLE®

Unscramble these four Jumbles, one letter to each square, to form four ordinary words.

YEGEL

ZIERP

LAVASS

TRUFOH

WHEN YOU INVITE
SOMEONE TO AN OUT-
RAGEOUSLY EXPENSIVE
RESTAURANT —

Now arrange the circled letters to form the surprise answer, as suggested by the above cartoon.

Print answer here   IT ☐☐☐☐☐☐☐ YOU ☐☐☐☐☐

JUMBLE®

Unscramble these four Jumbles, one letter
to each square, to form four ordinary words.

DEBIP

TOMIF

DOGOLY

GURFAL

THE INSOMNIAC
WAS ADVISED
TO SLEEP ON THE
EDGE OF HIS BED
IN ORDER TO DO
THIS WITHOUT DELAY.

Now arrange the circled letters to form
the surprise answer, as suggested by the
above cartoon.

Print answer here "☐☐☐☐☐ ☐☐☐"

JUMBLE®

Unscramble these four Jumbles, one letter
to each square, to form four ordinary words.

VOLEN

SIFIN

BASURD

SIPHOL

Bang

WHAT THE GUY WHO
JUST PRETENDED HE
WAS A GANGSTER
MUST HAVE BEEN.

Now arrange the circled letters to form
the surprise answer, as suggested by the
above cartoon.

Print answer here A "⃝⃝⃝⃝⃝ ⃝⃝⃝⃝"

JUMBLE®

Unscramble these four Jumbles, one letter
to each square, to form four ordinary words.

RYVEN

WHISS

TURIAL

SCYTIK

Wouldn't be caught
dead in them

WHAT SOME DECIDED TO
DO WHEN TROUSERS
FIRST BECAME
FASHIONABLE
FOR WOMEN.

Now arrange the circled letters to form
the surprise answer, as suggested by the
above cartoon.

**Print answer
here** ◯◯◯◯◯ THE ◯◯◯◯◯

JUMBLE®

Unscramble these four Jumbles, one letter
to each square, to form four ordinary words.

NARVE

IRROP

EMBLUH

PECDIT

THE BARBER TOLD
HIM STORIES THAT
COULD DO THIS.

Now arrange the circled letters to form
the surprise answer, as suggested by the
above cartoon.

Print answer here ⬡⬡⬡⬡⬡ HIS ⬡⬡⬡⬡

JUMBLE®

Unscramble these four Jumbles, one letter
to each square, to form four ordinary words.

KRYJE

DYPUG

TULNAW

YENNIT

Nobody goes there anymore

EATS

WHAT THE SLEAZY
RESTAURANT THAT
MADE THOSE AWFUL
SUBMARINE SAND-
WICHES DID.

Now arrange the circled letters to form
the surprise answer, as suggested by the
above cartoon.

Print answer here

JUMBLE®

Unscramble these four Jumbles, one letter to each square, to form four ordinary words.

IMNEC

CUPAN

KORSEM

SIMPOE

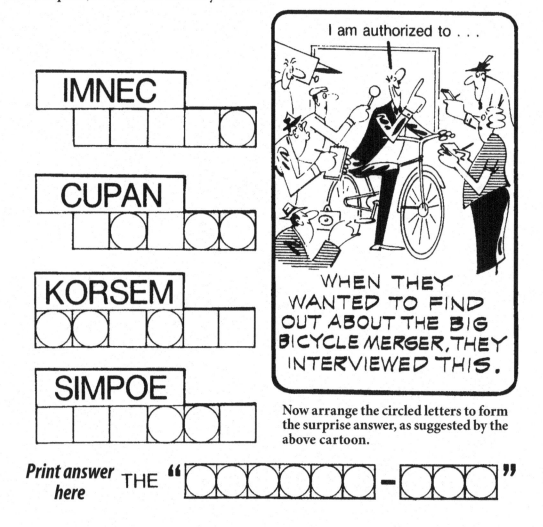

I am authorized to . . .

WHEN THEY WANTED TO FIND OUT ABOUT THE BIG BICYCLE MERGER, THEY INTERVIEWED THIS.

Now arrange the circled letters to form the surprise answer, as suggested by the above cartoon.

Print answer here THE " ◯◯◯◯◯◯ – ◯◯◯ "

JUMBLE

Unscramble these four Jumbles, one letter
to each square, to form four ordinary words.

VOYIR

TOINX

KLEECH

ETSAUL

WHY THE JUDGE
COULDN'T BE DIS-
TURBED AT DINNER.

Now arrange the circled letters to form
the surprise answer, as suggested by the
above cartoon.

**Print
answer
here**   HIS ☐☐☐☐☐ WAS "☐☐☐☐☐"
AT

JUMBLE®

Unscramble these four Jumbles, one letter to each square, to form four ordinary words.

OIXED

BOREP

GINENE

MADGEA

WHAT THE MAESTRO CALLED HIS ASSISTANT.

Now arrange the circled letters to form the surprise answer, as suggested by the above cartoon.

Print answer here HIS " ☐☐☐☐ ☐☐☐☐ "

JUMBLE®

Unscramble these four Jumbles, one letter to each square, to form four ordinary words.

ALLIC

THYAS

CYRIKT

YEMITS

WHAT THEY AGREED TO WHEN THEY OR- GANIZED THE CARD GAME ON THE PLANE.

Now arrange the circled letters to form the surprise answer, as suggested by the above cartoon.

Print answer here THE ◯◯◯'◯ THE ◯◯◯◯◯◯

JUMBLE

Unscramble these four Jumbles, one letter
to each square, to form four ordinary words.

BUIME

SHUBY

RATROM

TUGELL

ANOTHER NAME FOR
A PIRATE SHIP.

Now arrange the circled letters to form
the surprise answer, as suggested by the
above cartoon.

Print answer here A " ⬡⬡⬡⬡⬡ " ⬡⬡⬡⬡

JUMBLE®

Unscramble these four Jumbles, one letter
to each square, to form four ordinary words.

YONIR

PEXLE

POWDLE

YUGLIT

WHAT HAPPENED WHEN
THE PRICE OF DUCK
FEATHERS INCREASED?

Now arrange the circled letters to form
the surprise answer, as suggested by the
above cartoon.

Print answer here ◯◯◯◯◯ WENT ◯◯

JUMBLE®

Unscramble these four Jumbles, one letter to each square, to form four ordinary words.

CHEFT

ILLSE

LOWPAL

TAUNER

WHAT THAT PRIZE-WINNING DOG WAS.

Now arrange the circled letters to form the surprise answer, as suggested by the above cartoon.

Print answer here A ⬡⬡⬡⬡⬡ " ⬡⬡⬡ "

JUMBLE®

Unscramble these four Jumbles, one letter to each square, to form four ordinary words.

LITTE

ITTYD

DARZIL

OPEATT

WHAT THE GOSSIPY RATTLESNAKE WAS.

Now arrange the circled letters to form the surprise answer, as suggested by the above cartoon.

Print answer here   A ⃞⃞⃞⃞⃞⃞ " ⃞⃞⃞⃞ "

JUMBLE®

Unscramble these four Jumbles, one letter
to each square, to form four ordinary words.

WROPE

CLAWR

SHIVAL

INTYCE

WHAT THEY
CALLED THOSE
MOTORIZED NUTS.

Now arrange the circled letters to form
the surprise answer, as suggested by the
above cartoon.

Print answer
here "◯◯◯◯◯ – ◯◯◯◯◯"

JUMBLE®

Unscramble these four Jumbles, one letter to each square, to form four ordinary words.

ORNOH

DAULC

UNISCO

ALDLAB

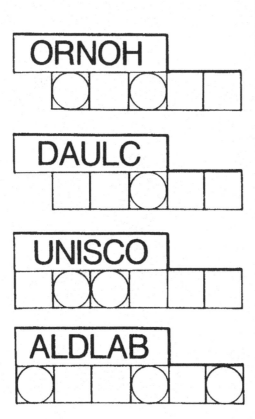

Doesn't recognize his old buddies

WHEN HE BECAME TOP BANANA HE LOST TOUCH WITH THIS.

Now arrange the circled letters to form the surprise answer, as suggested by the above cartoon.

Print answer here THE

JUMBLE®

Unscramble these four Jumbles, one letter to each square, to form four ordinary words.

ELVOH

MOIFT

DANAGE

RILIXE

I move a mistrial

A JURY NEVER WORKS RIGHT WHEN IT'S THIS.

Now arrange the circled letters to form the surprise answer, as suggested by the above cartoon.

Print answer here " ⬡⬡⬡⬡⬡ "

JUMBLE®

Unscramble these four Jumbles, one letter
to each square, to form four ordinary words.

PHARY

ISTUE

SEIBED

CORTER

We've all gone out. Your
food is in the refrigerator

WHAT SOME
PEOPLE'S HAND-
WRITING IS.

Now arrange the circled letters to form
the surprise answer, as suggested by the
above cartoon.

Print
answer
here

A " ⬡⬡⬡⬡⬡⬡ " ⬡⬡⬡⬡⬡

JUMBLE®

Unscramble these four Jumbles, one letter
to each square, to form four ordinary words.

BAWLY

MYLAD

HUBERC

ORFALL

WHAT THEY THOUGHT
IT WAS WHEN THE
WIMP TRIED TO ACT
LIKE A WOLF.

Now arrange the circled letters to form
the surprise answer, as suggested by the
above cartoon.

Print answer here ◯ " ◯◯◯◯ "

JUMBLE®

Unscramble these four Jumbles, one letter
to each square, to form four ordinary words.

HOPNY

CUSTO

FLUFEM

GETULL

WHERE'S THE
FENCING MASTER?

Now arrange the circled letters to form
the surprise answer, as suggested by the
above cartoon.

Print answer here ⬡⬡⬡ TO "⬡⬡⬡⬡⬡"

JUMBLE®

Unscramble these four Jumbles, one letter to each square, to form four ordinary words.

HINEW

PHLYS

SLYJUT

RARQUY

It's amazing how he comes up with them on the spur of the moment

WHAT THE STAND-UP COMEDIAN EQUIPS HIMSELF WITH.

Now arrange the circled letters to form the surprise answer, as suggested by the above cartoon.

Print answer here ⟨◯◯◯◯◯◯⟩

JUMBLE®

Unscramble these four Jumbles, one letter
to each square, to form four ordinary words.

YESTT

JAHAR

HOWALL

PYSEDE

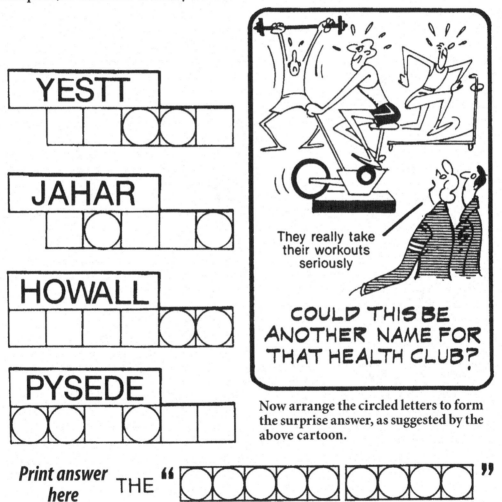

They really take
their workouts
seriously

COULD THIS BE
ANOTHER NAME FOR
THAT HEALTH CLUB?

Now arrange the circled letters to form
the surprise answer, as suggested by the
above cartoon.

Print answer here THE " ⃝⃝⃝⃝⃝⃝ ⃝⃝⃝⃝ "

JUMBLE®

Unscramble these four Jumbles, one letter
to each square, to form four ordinary words.

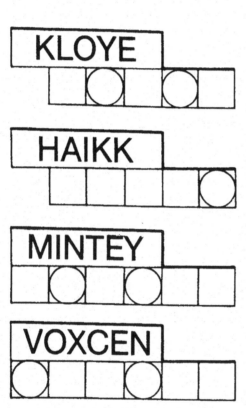

KLOYE

HAIKK

MINTEY

VOXCEN

THE ONLY VOICE
THAT DAD SOME-
TIMES HAS IN
FAMILY AFFAIRS.

Now arrange the circled letters to form
the surprise answer, as suggested by the
above cartoon.

Print answer here "  "

JUMBLE.

Unscramble these four Jumbles, one letter
to each square, to form four ordinary words.

SURBT

MILTI

CASMIO

FEETOF

Gee, it's
dark
tonight

WHAT DRACULA GOT
WHEN HE MISTOOK
A SNOWMAN FOR A
HUMAN BEING.

Now arrange the circled letters to form
the surprise answer, as suggested by the
above cartoon.

Print answer here

JUMBLE®

Unscramble these four Jumbles, one letter
to each square, to form four ordinary words.

VOARB
☐☐◯☐◯

TYDIT
☐◯☐◯☐

NINTTE
☐◯☐◯◯☐

RETTUL
◯☐☐◯☐☐

WHAT TO PAY
IF YOU DON'T WANT
TO SPEND TOO MUCH.

Now arrange the circled letters to form
the surprise answer, as suggested by the
above cartoon.

Print answer here ◯◯◯◯◯◯◯◯◯◯

JUMBLE®

Unscramble these four Jumbles, one letter to each square, to form four ordinary words.

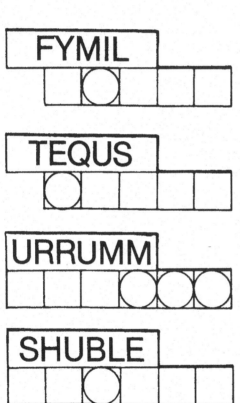

FYMIL

TEQUS

URRUMM

SHUBLE

HE DESERVES TO DO THIS WHEN HE BEHAVES LIKE A WORM.

Now arrange the circled letters to form the surprise answer, as suggested by the above cartoon.

Print answer here

91

JUMBLE®

Unscramble these four Jumbles, one letter
to each square, to form four ordinary words.

NAYRE

ERNIL

NATQUI

GINPTY

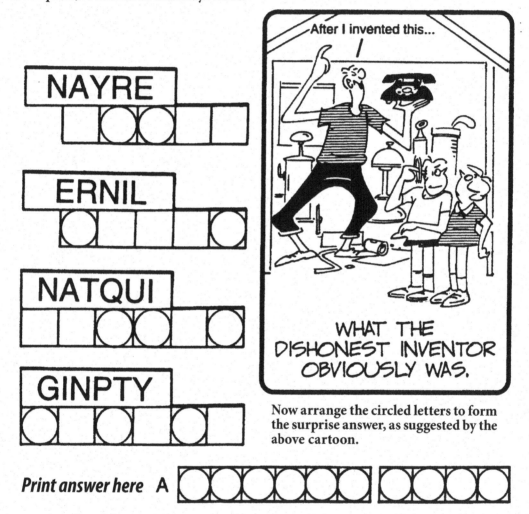

After I invented this...

WHAT THE
DISHONEST INVENTOR
OBVIOUSLY WAS.

Now arrange the circled letters to form
the surprise answer, as suggested by the
above cartoon.

Print answer here   A ⬡⬡⬡⬡⬡⬡ ⬡⬡⬡⬡

JUMBLE®

Unscramble these four Jumbles, one letter
to each square, to form four ordinary words.

CNOTH

NOUCE

KEPPUE

ICKEOO

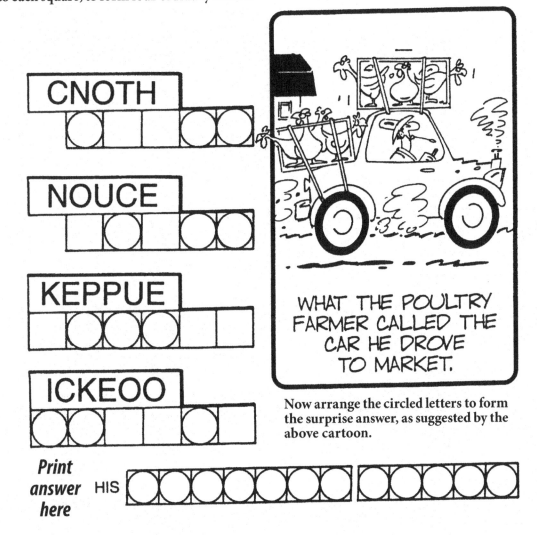

WHAT THE POULTRY
FARMER CALLED THE
CAR HE DROVE
TO MARKET.

Now arrange the circled letters to form
the surprise answer, as suggested by the
above cartoon.

Print
answer   HIS
here

JUMBLE®

Unscramble these four Jumbles, one letter to each square, to form four ordinary words.

TUCEA
◯◯◯◯◯◯

BEDAK
◯◯◯◯◯

RIDFOB
◯◯◯◯◯◯

TUNESA
◯◯◯◯◯◯

Only a half hour to go

WHAT THE TIRED MANAGER OF THE QUAINT INN LOOKED FORWARD TO.

Now arrange the circled letters to form the surprise answer, as suggested by the above cartoon.

Print answer here ◯◯◯ AND ◯◯◯◯◯◯◯◯◯◯

JUMBLE®

Unscramble these four Jumbles, one letter
to each square, to form four ordinary words.

EVVER

LAVIT

THECCI

GREATT

You're so cute

WHY MAGNETS
ARE FOUND ON
REFRIGERATORS.

Now arrange the circled letters to form
the surprise answer, as suggested by the
above cartoon.

*Print
answer
here* THEY'RE

95

JUMBLE®

Unscramble these four Jumbles, one letter
to each square, to form four ordinary words.

DEGAL

REQUE

GLEMIT

BOLIFE

Yeow!!

WHAT THE THIEF
GOT AT THE
COMPUTER STORE.

Now arrange the circled letters to form
the surprise answer, as suggested by the
above cartoon.

Print answer here A ☐☐☐☐☐ ☐☐☐☐☐

JUMBLE®

Unscramble these four Jumbles, one letter to each square, to form four ordinary words.

HERMY

DAANP

TRIOGE

SWETID

Taxes are too high!

You have to pay for services!

THE KIND OF CONVERSATION FOUND IN A BAR.

Now arrange the circled letters to form the surprise answer, as suggested by the above cartoon.

Print answer here

JUMBLE®

Unscramble these four Jumbles, one letter
to each square, to form four ordinary words.

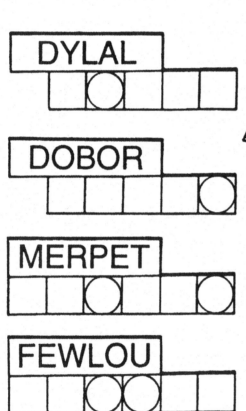

DYLAL

DOBOR

MERPET

FEWLOU

Honest--it was
somebody else!

WHAT THE
ART THIEF SAID
HE WAS.

Now arrange the circled letters to form
the surprise answer, as suggested by the
above cartoon.

Print answer here

JUMBLE®

Unscramble these four Jumbles, one letter
to each square, to form four ordinary words.

GOYGS

EXIDO

MYDOBE

DEFLAB

It's ours
now, dear

Let me get the
door for you

WHAT THE
SUCCESSFUL REALTOR
WAS KNOWN FOR.

Now arrange the circled letters to form
the surprise answer, as suggested by the
above cartoon.

*Print answer
here* HIS ⬡⬡⬡⬡ " ⬡⬡⬡⬡⬡ "

JUMBLE®

Unscramble these four Jumbles, one letter
to each square, to form four ordinary words.

ARRIB

OATAR

ENGLIT

GRAFEO

WHAT KIND OF
RELATIONSHIP THE
TWINS HAD IN
COLLEGE.

Now arrange the circled letters to form
the surprise answer, as suggested by the
above cartoon.

Print answer here

JUMBLE®

Unscramble these four Jumbles, one letter
to each square, to form four ordinary words.

GROOF

TYFFI

NIWWON

GIMLEN

The boss had a fight with his wife this morning

WHY THE WATCH-MAKER DIDN'T GET THE RAISE.

Now arrange the circled letters to form
the surprise answer, as suggested by the
above cartoon.

Print answer here HIS ⬡⬡⬡⬡⬡⬡ WAS ⬡⬡⬡

101

JUMBLE®

Unscramble these four Jumbles, one letter
to each square, to form four ordinary words.

YALFE

CINEE

LUSSTY

SMURTE

Thank you,
next

WHAT NEW ACTORS
BECOME A PART OF.

Now arrange the circled letters to form
the surprise answer, as suggested by the
above cartoon.

Print answer here THE ⬡⬡⬡⬡ ⬡⬡⬡⬡⬡⬡

102

JUMBLE®

Unscramble these four Jumbles, one letter
to each square, to form four ordinary words.

MUHTB

AAKKY

PRIGSN

NAPEDX

Are you
getting any
better?

It won't
go away.

THE HULA DANCER WAS
REALLY SICK. SHE HAD
A BAD COLD AND SHE
COULDN'T ----

Now arrange the circled letters to form
the surprise answer, as suggested by the
above cartoon.

Print answer here

JUMBLE®

Unscramble these four Jumbles, one letter
to each square, to form four ordinary words.

HYYLS

ROLYG

BEMLIN

DONEOL

Howdy!

They're so
friendly.

Sam loves
the horses.

THEY BOUGHT THE HOUSE
NEXT TO THE HORSE FARM
BECAUSE THEY LOVED
THE ---

Now arrange the circled letters to form
the surprise answer, as suggested by the
above cartoon.

Print answer " ⬡⬡⬡⬡⬡ - ⬡⬡⬡⬡ "
here

JUMBLE®

Unscramble these four Jumbles, one letter
to each square, to form four ordinary words.

GAMIE

DORPO

RENYRO

WULLAF

I love just floating here.

This is a great setup.

THE FROG COULDN'T BUILD
A DECK WHERE HE LIVED, BUT
HE WAS ABLE TO MAKE A ----

Now arrange the circled letters to form
the surprise answer, as suggested by the
above cartoon.

Print answer here " ⬡⬡⬡⬡⬡ "

JUMBLE®

Unscramble these four Jumbles, one letter to each square, to form four ordinary words.

TIXSY

EESSN

EPUPIL

YARNTT

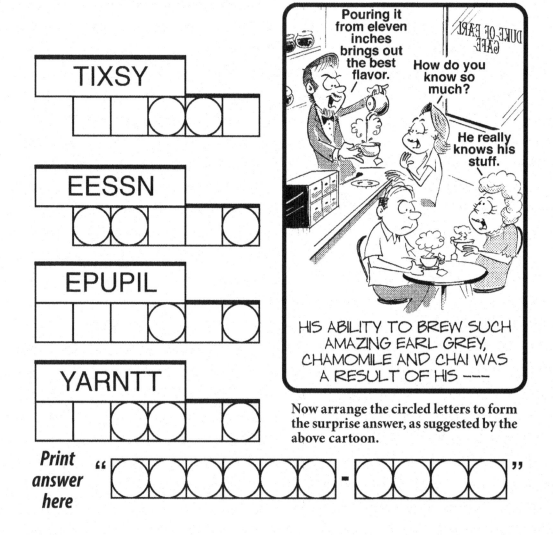

Pouring it from eleven inches brings out the best flavor.

How do you know so much?

He really knows his stuff.

DUKE OF EARL CAFÉ

HIS ABILITY TO BREW SUCH AMAZING EARL GREY, CHAMOMILE AND CHAI WAS A RESULT OF HIS ---

Now arrange the circled letters to form the surprise answer, as suggested by the above cartoon.

Print answer here

" ◯◯◯◯◯◯ - ◯◯◯◯ "

106

JUMBLE®

Unscramble these four Jumbles, one letter to each square, to form four ordinary words.

MAFYO

SHISW

FEUDON

TRIVED

AFTER A COMPETING LEMONADE SELLER MOVED IN NEXT TO HER, SHE WAS ----

Now arrange the circled letters to form the surprise answer, as suggested by the above cartoon.

Print answer here

JUMBLE®

Unscramble these four Jumbles, one letter
to each square, to form four ordinary words.

DRAYT

CINEE

KANEEW

TOATOT

WHEN THE CARTOONIST
SKETCHED THE WHITE
HOUSE GUARD, HE ----

Now arrange the circled letters to form
the surprise answer, as suggested by the
above cartoon.

Print answer here

JUMBLE®

Unscramble these four Jumbles, one letter to each square, to form four ordinary words.

RIROG

DAGLE

GARNDO

SOCTLE

Now arrange the circled letters to form the surprise answer, as suggested by the above cartoon.

Print answer here " ◯◯◯◯◯ " ◯◯◯◯◯◯◯◯◯

JUMBLE®

Unscramble these four Jumbles, one letter
to each square, to form four ordinary words.

KISYR

MEASU

CONSIA

TEULTO

The
Write Stuff

Letter
Paper

Notebooks
2 for 1

All Pens
Must Go!

AFTER THE STATIONERY
STORE CLOSED FOR THE
EVENING, EVERYTHING
WAS ---

Now arrange the circled letters to form
the surprise answer, as suggested by the
above cartoon.

Print
answer
here

JUMBLE®

Unscramble these four Jumbles, one letter to each square, to form four ordinary words.

PEMTT

OORDE

RUTFOH

MURYCM

Now, the two inline-four engines share a common crankshaft. This V8 has a somewhat more complex crossplane crankshaft with heavy counterweights to eliminate the vibrations.

I just asked what you had for lunch.

THE MECHANIC WHO LOVED TO TALK ABOUT ENGINES WAS A ---

Now arrange the circled letters to form the surprise answer, as suggested by the above cartoon.

Print answer here

JUMBLE®

Unscramble these four Jumbles, one letter to each square, to form four ordinary words.

IBEDA

WRLIT

NIRCUH

SENLOS

So, how's your hot dog? Do you love it?

It's OK. I can't believe he only had mustard.

Mean Mr. Mustard's Hot Dogs

THE HOT DOG WAS OK, BUT HE REALLY WISHED HE COULD HAVE ----

Now arrange the circled letters to form the surprise answer, as suggested by the above cartoon.

Print answer here

JUMBLE®

Unscramble these four Jumbles, one letter
to each square, to form four ordinary words.

LEWDL

NAHYD

MZYEEN

ANKAWE

Can you beat
Tire Tower's
price?

TOM'S
TIRES
We'll keep
you Rolling!

Of course!
I'll also throw
in an alignment,
rotation, and a
free spare.

SHE NEEDED NEW TIRES FOR
HER CAR, AND THE TIRE
SALESMAN WAS READY TO ---

Now arrange the circled letters to form
the surprise answer, as suggested by the
above cartoon.

**Print
answer
here**

JUMBLE®

Unscramble these four Jumbles, one letter to each square, to form four ordinary words.

LOGIO

DUOIA

MEBREM

CINEYL

How's it feel to be one of the richest people in the world?

That's the biggest piece of gold I've ever seen!

AFTER THEY STRUCK GOLD, THE OWNER OF THE GOLD MINE WAS A ----

Now arrange the circled letters to form the surprise answer, as suggested by the above cartoon.

Print answer here " ☐☐☐☐☐☐☐☐ - ☐☐☐☐ "

114

JUMBLE®

Unscramble these four Jumbles, one letter to each square, to form four ordinary words.

COLKB

NOREP

CABENO

NICORI

WHEN IT CAME TO ANSWERING QUESTIONS ABOUT HIS NEW NOVEL, THE AUTHOR WAS AN ----

Now arrange the circled letters to form the surprise answer, as suggested by the above cartoon.

Print answer here

JUMBLE®

Unscramble these four Jumbles, one letter
to each square, to form four ordinary words.

FALWU

GAMIE

LTUNAF

DOGINI

I thought I was
getting the
Porsche!

It's final.
Everything
goes to
charity.

Honey, I
thought
you were
leaving
me
every-
thing?

Not a
chance.

HIS HEIRS ALL WANTED
A PIECE OF HIS FORTUNE,
BUT HE WAS ----

Now arrange the circled letters to form
the surprise answer, as suggested by the
above cartoon.

Print answer here

JUMBLE

Unscramble these four Jumbles, one letter to each square, to form four ordinary words.

LIRDL

CLUPK

MURSEM

TETAMU

THE TUG-OF-WAR
WAS GOING WELL
UNTIL HE ----

Now arrange the circled letters to form the surprise answer, as suggested by the above cartoon.

Print answer here

JUMBLE®

Unscramble these four Jumbles, one letter to each square, to form four ordinary words.

ZOYDO

YOLRA

NIWOWD

BUSTIM

... I know I can trust you.

Your secret's safe with me.

HE TOLD CASPER THE GHOST HIS SECRET BECAUSE HE KNEW CASPER ---

Now arrange the circled letters to form the surprise answer, as suggested by the above cartoon.

Print answer here

◯◯◯◯◯◯ ' ◯   ◯◯◯   ◯◯◯

JUMBLE®

Unscramble these four Jumbles, one letter to each square, to form four ordinary words.

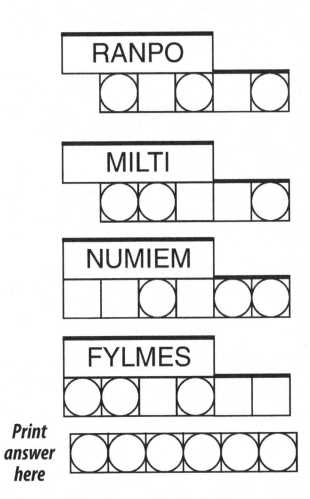

RANPO

MILTI

NUMIEM

FYLMES

I can't believe you finished ahead of schedule.

Everything went like clockwork.

INSTALLATION OF THE NEW CLOCK WAS COMPLETED IN A ----

Now arrange the circled letters to form the surprise answer, as suggested by the above cartoon.

Print answer here

JUMBLE®

Unscramble these four Jumbles, one letter
to each square, to form four ordinary words.

PALAH

RIWTL

KOLTEC

VHALIS

Why isn't this
50% off? Unless I
get that discount,
I'm not buying
anything.

Sorry, the
jewelry is
25% off.

50%
OFF

25%
off

THE SHOPPER DEMANDED
50% OFF EVERYTHING IN
THE STORE BECAUSE
SHE WANTED TO ----

Now arrange the circled letters to form
the surprise answer, as suggested by the
above cartoon.

Print
answer
here

" ⬡⬡⬡⬡⬡ " ⬡⬡ ⬡⬡⬡

JUMBLE®

Unscramble these four Jumbles, one letter to each square, to form four ordinary words.

UNMOD

FINSF

LYALGE

SPYMAW

THE WATERFOWL'S FINAL PERFORMANCE WAS HER ———

Now arrange the circled letters to form the surprise answer, as suggested by the above cartoon.

Print answer here

JUMBLE®

Unscramble these four Jumbles, one letter
to each square, to form four ordinary words.

THEYF

KAHIK

LUWSAR

TINKET

It's from his
Mongolian
barbecue
period.

Do you think
I'm a fool?
He didn't paint
this.

PICASSO

HE SAID THE PAINTING OF THE
MONGOLIAN LEADER WAS A
PICASSO, BUT IT WAS
MADE BY A ----

Now arrange the circled letters to form
the surprise answer, as suggested by the
above cartoon.

Print
answer
here

" ◯◯◯◯ "   ◯◯◯◯◯◯

JUMBLE®

Unscramble these four Jumbles, one letter to each square, to form four ordinary words.

NUTTS

NEESS

DONELO

LACELO

There are so many to choose from.

They have 30 sites available in both phases.

PHASE 1   PHASE 2

MODEL HOME

WHEN IT CAME TO PLACES TO BUILD A HOME, THE NEW SUBDIVISION HAD ----

Now arrange the circled letters to form the surprise answer, as suggested by the above cartoon.

Print answer here

JUMBLE®

Unscramble these four Jumbles, one letter to each square, to form four ordinary words.

LAPNT

REHUS

BRIFDO

XILIER

Make another steady orbit above the planet, Mr. Data.

Aye aye, sir.

THE SPACESHIP'S ORBIT ENCIRCLING THE PLANET WAS A ---

Now arrange the circled letters to form the surprise answer, as suggested by the above cartoon.

Print answer here

JUMBLE®

Unscramble these four Jumbles, one letter to each square, to form four ordinary words.

REXET

GINAA

NESOSA

NASLOM

Holy cow. You're fit.

You should try pulling a plow once in a while.

THE BULL WOULD LOSE THE ARM-WRESTLING MATCH BECAUSE HE WASN'T ----

Now arrange the circled letters to form the surprise answer, as suggested by the above cartoon.

Print answer here

JUMBLE®

Unscramble these four Jumbles, one letter
to each square, to form four ordinary words.

COREF

GEMAO

DINKUN

NCAATV

It was
the last
one they
had.

It's
perfect.

TO TRANSPORT HIS
COWS, THE FARMER
RENTED A ----

Now arrange the circled letters to form
the surprise answer, as suggested by the
above cartoon.

*Print
answer
here*

" ◯◯◯ - ◯◯◯◯◯ " ◯◯◯◯◯

JUMBLE®

Unscramble these four Jumbles, one letter to each square, to form four ordinary words.

VODIA

TOTEC

DROFIB

GLOONB

Whoa! This is the best one I've seen.

In my expert opinion, I'd say it's three days old.

SASQUATCH WAS EASY TO TRACK BECAUSE HE HAD A ----

Now arrange the circled letters to form the surprise answer, as suggested by the above cartoon.

Print answer here ◯◯◯ ◯◯◯◯

JUMBLE®

Unscramble these four Jumbles, one letter
to each square, to form four ordinary words.

NORTF

SACEE

LAIHEW

RIPSLA

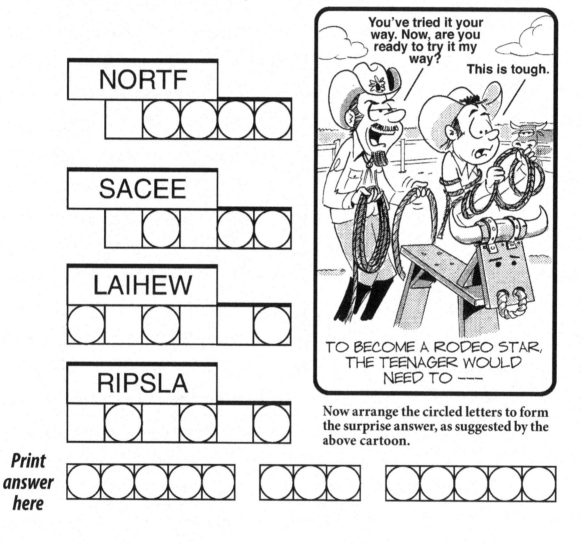

You've tried it your way. Now, are you ready to try it my way?

This is tough.

TO BECOME A RODEO STAR,
THE TEENAGER WOULD
NEED TO ---

Now arrange the circled letters to form
the surprise answer, as suggested by the
above cartoon.

Print
answer
here

JUMBLE®

Unscramble these four Jumbles, one letter
to each square, to form four ordinary words.

CPOMH

LATYL

DALEDO

CCANEH

I need it to be reliable.
I'm not looking to
spend a lot of gold.

I have a
deal for
you.

DEAL

LOW
MILAGE

WHEN KING ARTHUR WENT
TO THE DESERT,
HE VISITED THE ----

Now arrange the circled letters to form
the surprise answer, as suggested by the
above cartoon.

**Print answer
here**

129

JUMBLE®

Unscramble these four Jumbles, one letter
to each square, to form four ordinary words.

MUFRO

FHSAL

SWIDON

TOATOT

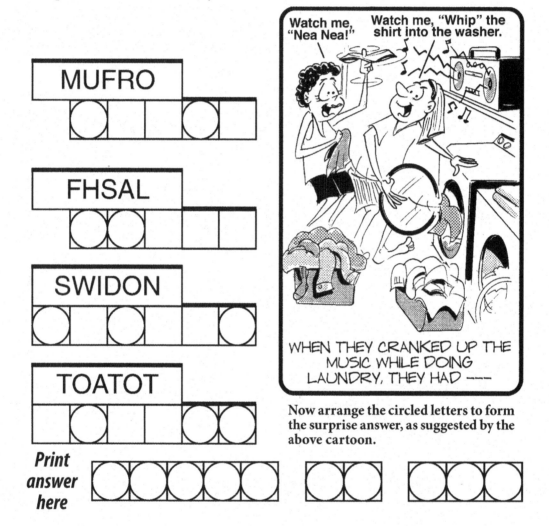

Watch me,
"Nea Nea!"

Watch me, "Whip" the
shirt into the washer.

WHEN THEY CRANKED UP THE
MUSIC WHILE DOING
LAUNDRY, THEY HAD ----

Now arrange the circled letters to form
the surprise answer, as suggested by the
above cartoon.

Print
answer
here

JUMBLE®

Unscramble these four Jumbles, one letter
to each square, to form four ordinary words.

GIBEE

ROPAN

LACCEK

GHRACE

All I'm saying is that you need to eat less meat.

Okay. I'll try a slice of cheese.

Hey! I was just talking about you, man.

JOHN LENNON WASN'T CERTAIN
HE'D LIKE THE PIZZA, BUT HE
DECIDED TO GIVE THE ----

Now arrange the circled letters to form
the surprise answer, as suggested by the
above cartoon.

Print answer here " ◯◯◯◯◯ " ◯ ◯◯◯◯◯◯◯

131

JUMBLE®

Unscramble these four Jumbles, one letter
to each square, to form four ordinary words.

RIWEP

BODUT

SWIMDO

GANTLE

This doesn't
taste like a
Seabreeze.

Hey! This drink
isn't strong
enough.

The
S.AND.
BAR

It's the way
I always
make them.

THE DRINKS AT THE
UNDERSEA BAR WERE ----

Now arrange the circled letters to form
the surprise answer, as suggested by the
above cartoon.

Print
answer
here

JUMBLE®

Unscramble these four Jumbles, one letter to each square, to form four ordinary words.

CIMMI

OMYNE

GAMENA

SALWEE

Look at them go!

They're naturals!

WHEN THEY TAUGHT THEIR PUPPIES HOW TO DOG PADDLE, THINGS WENT ----

Now arrange the circled letters to form the surprise answer, as suggested by the above cartoon.

Print answer here

JUMBLE®

Unscramble these four Jumbles, one letter to each square, to form four ordinary words.

DOMME

RUBOR

NYRCAN

FLAMEE

THE ATTENDANT WAS WELL-LIKED AND EFFICIENT. THEY LOVED HIS ----

Now arrange the circled letters to form the surprise answer, as suggested by the above cartoon.

Print answer here

JUMBLE®

Unscramble these four Jumbles, one letter to each square, to form four ordinary words.

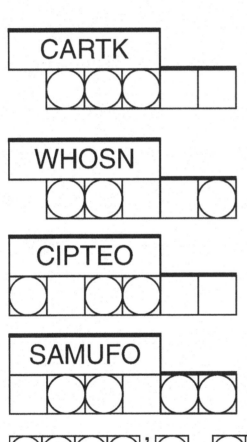

CARTK

WHOSN

CIPTEO

SAMUFO

I have some swell news for you George. You got the part!

Are you pulling my leg?

TELEPHONE

Get your paper here!

WHEN GEORGE REEVES GOT THE ROLE OF CLARK KENT ON TV, HE SAID ——

Now arrange the circled letters to form the surprise answer, as suggested by the above cartoon.

Print answer here

◯◯◯◯'◯ ◯◯◯◯◯, ◯◯◯

JUMBLE®

Unscramble these four Jumbles, one letter to each square, to form four ordinary words.

AROCK

CYYKU

BONKER

UTEDPA

Oh! Can I give your poker game a try?

All you need is money.

Be our guest.

HE ASKED IF HE COULD JOIN THEIR POKER GAME, AND THEY SAID ----

Now arrange the circled letters to form the surprise answer, as suggested by the above cartoon.

Print answer here

JUMBLE®

Unscramble these four Jumbles, one letter to each square, to form four ordinary words.

NUDMO

SIPEO

DOLUME

RIRTEW

Now, I want you to try our Pinot.

POP YOUR CORK

You have such a great variety here.

THEY SOLD AND SAMPLED A WIDE VARIETY OF WINES. CUSTOMERS LOVED THE ---

Now arrange the circled letters to form the surprise answer, as suggested by the above cartoon.

Print answer here " ⬡⬡-⬡⬡⬡⬡-⬡⬡⬡ "

JUMBLE®

Unscramble these four Jumbles, one letter
to each square, to form four ordinary words.

RIGBN

GOCLI

FUXSIF

SENUGI

WHEN THE ALIENS LANDED
ON THE HIGHWAY,
THEY SAW ---

Now arrange the circled letters to form
the surprise answer, as suggested by the
above cartoon.

Print
answer
here

JUMBLE®

Unscramble these four Jumbles, one letter to each square, to form four ordinary words.

CERKW

GIBEE

VAHENE

CHERNW

Dad, is that you?

Yep. I was much larger at the time your mom and I started dating.

You've done a great job of keeping the pounds off all these years.

HE WAS
100 POUNDS
HEAVIER ----

Now arrange the circled letters to form the surprise answer, as suggested by the above cartoon.

Print answer here

" ◯◯◯◯◯ " ◯◯◯◯ ◯◯◯◯

JUMBLE®

Unscramble these four Jumbles, one letter
to each square, to form four ordinary words.

HCOVU

CLEET

SOLONE

OSANES

This type of
wood needs
a week to
straighten
out.

I thought
you knew
how to
build a
deck!

Is this
safe?

WHEN THE DECK BUILDER TOLD
THEM HE DID HIGH-QUALITY
WORK, HE WASN'T BEING ----

Now arrange the circled letters to form
the surprise answer, as suggested by the
above cartoon.

Print
answer
here

JUMBLE®

Unscramble these four Jumbles, one letter to each square, to form four ordinary words.

ITPEN

CERYM

HATURO

TYACCH

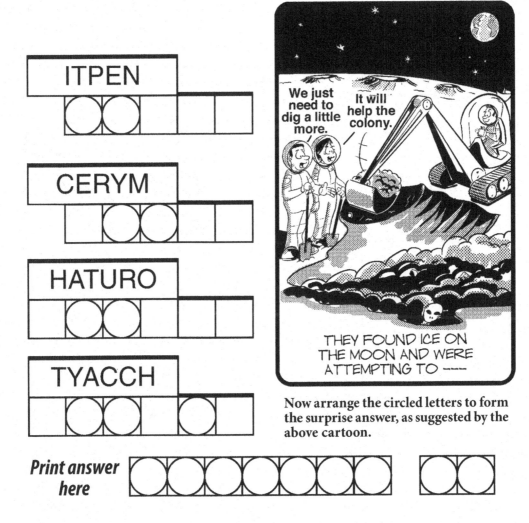

We just need to dig a little more.

It will help the colony.

THEY FOUND ICE ON THE MOON AND WERE ATTEMPTING TO ----

Now arrange the circled letters to form the surprise answer, as suggested by the above cartoon.

Print answer here ◯◯◯◯◯◯◯ ◯◯

JUMBLE

Unscramble these four Jumbles, one letter
to each square, to form four ordinary words.

SKIRB

FYCAN

LIESAY

DUGETG

Way to go!
I'm so happy
for you.

AFTER WEIGHING HERSELF,
AND SEEING SHE'D LOST
50 POUNDS, SHE HAD A ----

Now arrange the circled letters to form
the surprise answer, as suggested by the
above cartoon.

Print
answer
here

JUMBLE®

Unscramble these four Jumbles, one letter
to each square, to form four ordinary words.

LOGIO

SMOTP

GUCATH

BOWLEB

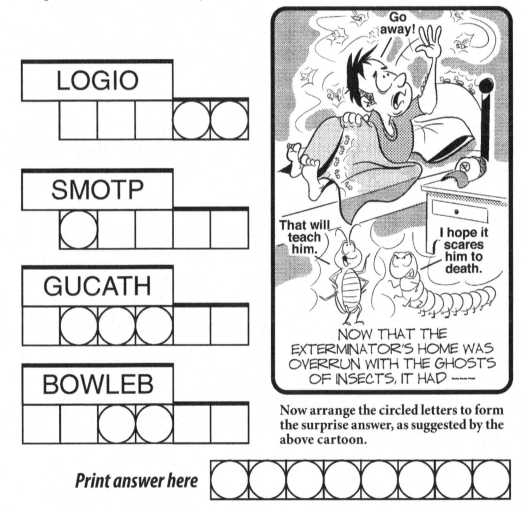

Go away!

That will teach him.

I hope it scares him to death.

NOW THAT THE
EXTERMINATOR'S HOME WAS
OVERRUN WITH THE GHOSTS
OF INSECTS, IT HAD ----

Now arrange the circled letters to form
the surprise answer, as suggested by the
above cartoon.

Print answer here

JUMBLE®

Unscramble these four Jumbles, one letter
to each square, to form four ordinary words.

SUHEO

GIBON

HYAMME

VIRRED

They feel much better!

These will be worth the hassle.

HE REPLACED HIS HORSE'S SHOES BECAUSE IT ----

Now arrange the circled letters to form
the surprise answer, as suggested by the
above cartoon.

Print answer here

JUMBLE®

Unscramble these four Jumbles, one letter to each square, to form four ordinary words.

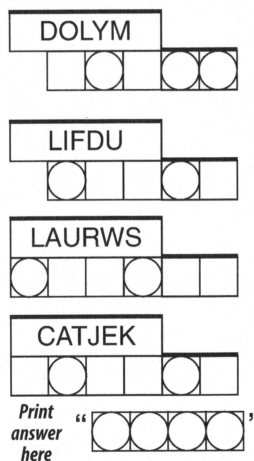

DOLYM

LIFDU

LAURWS

CATJEK

After you! You have beautiful horses.

HE SLOWED DOWN FOR THE PEOPLE ON THE HORSES BECAUSE THEY HAD THE ----

Now arrange the circled letters to form the surprise answer, as suggested by the above cartoon.

Print answer here

" "

JUMBLE®

Unscramble these four Jumbles, one letter to each square, to form four ordinary words.

FYMIL

FYITF

CENBOK

ROXVET

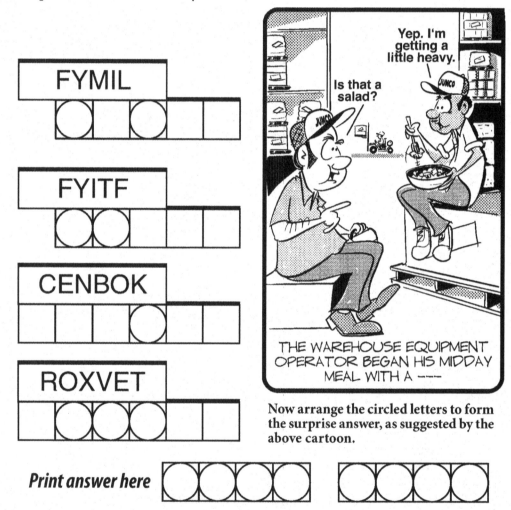

Is that a salad?

Yep. I'm getting a little heavy.

THE WAREHOUSE EQUIPMENT OPERATOR BEGAN HIS MIDDAY MEAL WITH A ---

Now arrange the circled letters to form the surprise answer, as suggested by the above cartoon.

Print answer here

146

JUMBLE®

Unscramble these four Jumbles, one letter
to each square, to form four ordinary words.

ILTIM

BOHYB

NENEVU

SGOTOE

Great big
globs of
greasy, grimy,
gopher guts!
You're going
down,
varmint!

THE GREENSKEEPER
WAS UPSET WHEN A
GOPHER MADE A ---

Now arrange the circled letters to form
the surprise answer, as suggested by the
above cartoon.

*Print
answer
here*

⬚⬚⬚⬚ ⬚⬚ ⬚⬚⬚

JUMBLE®

Unscramble these four Jumbles, one letter
to each square, to form four ordinary words.

LRUBT

KALYE

BEMMEL

DARWIN

That's so fake!
You can't fool
them with that.

You're wrong!
This is the only
way to catch the
big ones.

WHEN IT CAME TO WHETHER
WORMS OR LURES ATTRACT
MORE FISH, IT WAS ----

Now arrange the circled letters to form
the surprise answer, as suggested by the
above cartoon.

Print
answer
here

" ⬚⬚-⬚⬚⬚⬚-⬚⬚⬚⬚ "

JUMBLE®

Unscramble these four Jumbles, one letter
to each square, to form four ordinary words.

SERDS

UDUNE

ARPSIN

GATEEN

WHEN ANDREW JOHNSON WAS
IMPEACHED ON FEB. 24, 1868,
IT WAS ----

Now arrange the circled letters to form
the surprise answer, as suggested by the
above cartoon.

Print
answer
here

" ⬡⬡-⬡⬡⬡⬡⬡⬡⬡⬡⬡-⬡⬡ "

JUMBLE®

Unscramble these four Jumbles, one letter to each square, to form four ordinary words.

HOBTO

ZIDYZ

LAMCYL

CALEHB

This is grass! I can't eat this!

You'll love this!

THE PANDA WANTED TO BUY THE WORLD'S FASTEST GROWING PLANT, BUT HE WAS BEING ----

Now arrange the circled letters to form the surprise answer, as suggested by the above cartoon.

Print answer here

150

JUMBLE®

Unscramble these four Jumbles, one letter
to each square, to form four ordinary words.

KIDYN

ZOYDO

KAHNES

GOLANO

She's the best.

Thank you.

Let's spread your fingers a little more.

WHEN IT CAME TO LEARNING
SIGN LANGUAGE, THE
STUDENT WAS ———

Now arrange the circled letters to form
the surprise answer, as suggested by the
above cartoon.

Print
answer
here

JUMBLE®

Unscramble these four Jumbles, one letter
to each square, to form four ordinary words.

CRIBH

TYPTU

MORHEC

PEXMET

Do we
have
money for
a new bike
path?

What's our
budget for
next year?

I say we
purchase a
new
gazebo.

WHEN THE TOWN NEEDED TO
MAKE BIG PURCHASES, IT HAD
TO BE HANDLED ----

Now arrange the circled letters to form
the surprise answer, as suggested by the
above cartoon.

Print
answer
here

" ◯◯◯ " ◯◯◯◯◯◯◯◯◯◯

JUMBLE®

Unscramble these four Jumbles, one letter
to each square, to form four ordinary words.

SUDEO

TUBRS

MOSTOH

DUNEFO

I don't think
we're going to
be able to plant
these.

This is too
tough.

TRYING TO PLANT
FLOWERS IN THE ROCKY
SOIL WAS ----

Now arrange the circled letters to form
the surprise answer, as suggested by the
above cartoon.

*Print
answer
here*

JUMBLE®

Unscramble these four Jumbles, one letter
to each square, to form four ordinary words.

LOTCH

DABIE

DBRUSA

REGFTO

Well, crawl faster!

Quit following me so closely!

THE REPTILES HAD PROBLEMS
COMMUTING IN THE EVERGLADES
BECAUSE OF THE ----

Now arrange the circled letters to form
the surprise answer, as suggested by the
above cartoon.

Print
answer
here

" ⬡⬡⬡⬡ - ⬡⬡⬡⬡⬡⬡ "

154

JUMBLE®

Unscramble these four Jumbles, one letter
to each square, to form four ordinary words.

IOONN

PUREP

GUTGEN

RUCACE

Our past history
has shown we can
accomplish this.

Drop the word,
"past." It's
redundant.

BEFORE HER UPCOMING
SPEECH TO THE LEGISLATURE,
THE SENATOR DID MUCH ----

Now arrange the circled letters to form
the surprise answer, as suggested by the
above cartoon.

Print
answer
here

"◯◯◯◯ - ◯◯◯◯◯◯◯◯"

JUMBLE®

Unscramble these four Jumbles, one letter
to each square, to form four ordinary words.

ORPGU

RWONB

LICOSA

CTIWEK

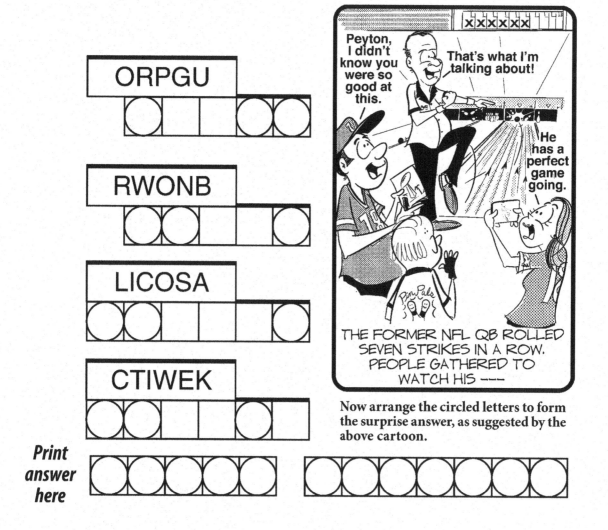

Peyton,
I didn't
know you
were so
good at
this.

That's what I'm
talking about!

He
has a
perfect
game
going.

THE FORMER NFL QB ROLLED
SEVEN STRIKES IN A ROW.
PEOPLE GATHERED TO
WATCH HIS ---

Now arrange the circled letters to form
the surprise answer, as suggested by the
above cartoon.

*Print
answer
here*

JUMBLE®

Unscramble these four Jumbles, one letter
to each square, to form four ordinary words.

CHKEC

TAYNG

MUNSOM

PREETW

THE COSMETOLOGY
STUDENT MISSED HER EXAM
AND NEEDED TO TAKE A ----

Now arrange the circled letters to form
the surprise answer, as suggested by the
above cartoon.

*Print
answer
here*

JUMBLE®

Unscramble these four Jumbles, one letter to each square, to form four ordinary words.

KENTA

SUYFS

VESIDT

NOOTCT

Can we get a break if we pay cash?

How about 10% off?

Sorry, no deals.

$15/ft

THEY WERE HOPING TO GET A DISCOUNT ON A GRANITE COUNTERTOP, BUT THE PRICE WAS ----

Now arrange the circled letters to form the surprise answer, as suggested by the above cartoon.

Print answer here

JUMBLE®

Unscramble these four Jumbles, one letter
to each square, to form four ordinary words.

AMEGI

ENOKT

CERTNH

OCONUP

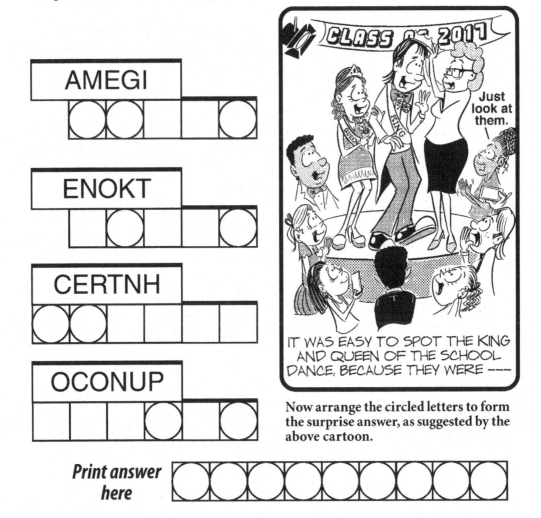

Just
look at
them.

IT WAS EASY TO SPOT THE KING
AND QUEEN OF THE SCHOOL
DANCE, BECAUSE THEY WERE ---

Now arrange the circled letters to form
the surprise answer, as suggested by the
above cartoon.

**Print answer
here**

159

JUMBLE®

Unscramble these four Jumbles, one letter
to each square, to form four ordinary words.

DANYH

VEEWA

BREEKU

NOCHES

At least my ale comes from organic hops.

Mine doesn't taste like a pine tree, like yours.

WHEN THE BEER MAKERS ARGUED OVER WHO MADE BETTER BEER, THE RESULT WAS A ---

Now arrange the circled letters to form
the surprise answer, as suggested by the
above cartoon.

Print answer here " ⬡⬡⬡⬡⬡ - ⬡⬡⬡⬡ "

JUMBLE®

Unscramble these four Jumbles, one letter to each square, to form four ordinary words.

TAHEW

NUCTO

SWODAH

HEGTWI

No more matching clothes.

Well, at least I can tell you apart now.

THE IDENTICAL TWIN BOYS DRESSED SO DIFFERENTLY BECAUSE ----

Now arrange the circled letters to form the surprise answer, as suggested by the above cartoon.

Print answer here

" ◯◯◯ " ◯◯◯◯◯ ◯◯◯ ◯◯◯

161

JUMBLE®

Unscramble these four Jumbles, one letter to each square, to form four ordinary words.

YTEPT

SOKKI

UNMEHA

RICCSU

HE WOULDN'T STOP COMPLAINING ABOUT THE WINE, SO HIS WIFE WANTED HIM TO ---

Now arrange the circled letters to form the surprise answer, as suggested by the above cartoon.

Print answer here

JUMBLE®
Birthday

Challenger
Puzzles

JUMBLE

Unscramble these six Jumbles, one letter
to each square, to form six ordinary words.

FASTIE

UNGOTE

REEBOF

YEMITS

CYTHAC

TELPOI

REAL ESTATE

You now have full title to the house

DEED

YOU MIGHT HAVE A
VESTED INTEREST
IN THIS!

Now arrange the circled letters
to form the surprise answer, as
suggested by the above cartoon.

*Print
answer
here*

A ☐☐☐☐☐☐ - ☐☐☐☐☐ ☐☐☐☐

JUMBLE®

Unscramble these six Jumbles, one letter to each square, to form six ordinary words.

WECHEN

BOLGEN

SMIDOH

USEBUD

LOSFIS

ENLOUG

WHAT A GOOD BODY SNATCHER WOULDN'T BE WITHOUT ON A NIGHT LIKE THIS.

Now arrange the circled letters to form the surprise answer, as suggested by the above cartoon.

Print answer here   HIS   "⬡⬡⬡⬡⬡-⬡⬡⬡⬡⬡"

JUMBLE®

Unscramble these six Jumbles, one letter
to each square, to form six ordinary words.

TRAWEY

FELBAF

YORCAN

GEOVAY

DEMANT

ENGINS

I refuse to
answer on the grounds . . .
(yak yak yak)

He doesn't say
much but he has
a tough
reputation

WHAT YOU WOULDN'T
EXPECT TO GET
FROM A MAN OF
FEW WORDS.

Now arrange the circled letters
to form the surprise answer, as
suggested by the above cartoon.

Print answer **A**
here

JUMBLE®

Unscramble these six Jumbles, one letter to each square, to form six ordinary words.

BELMIN

DUNOAL

NUTTOB

BLANEE

KRILLE

SHENOC

My dear, you'll never guess what I saw going on between the mermaid and . . .

WHAT THE TALKATIVE WHALE WAS.

Now arrange the circled letters to form the surprise answer, as suggested by the above cartoon.

Print answer here **BIG**

167

JUMBLE®

Unscramble these six Jumbles, one letter to each square, to form six ordinary words.

JINNOE

ROPPEH

SMARDI

LOUBES

GIZZAG

YINTTE

So long

Last drinks

AT A PLACE LIKE THIS
EXPECT THEM AT
CLOSING TIME.

Now arrange the circled letters to form the surprise answer, as suggested by the above cartoon.

Print answer here

JUMBLE®

Unscramble these six Jumbles, one letter
to each square, to form six ordinary words.

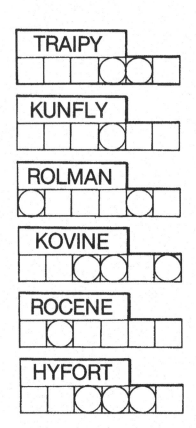

TRAIPY

KUNFLY

ROLMAN

KOVINE

ROCENE

HYFORT

WHAT WOULD YOU SAY IF
THE SEA DRIED UP?

Now arrange the circled letters
to form the surprise answer, as
suggested by the above cartoon.

Print
answer
here

" WE ⬡⬡⬡⬡⬡ " ⬡ A ⬡⬡⬡⬡⬡⬡ "

JUMBLE®

Unscramble these six Jumbles, one letter
to each square, to form six ordinary words.

VIYLE

SCOMAT

GRANDO

STEMOD

REESHA

TAPECK

They say he's
the best!

MD

WHAT AN
OPHTHALMOLOGIST'S
OFFICE IS.

Now arrange the circled letters to form
the surprise answer, as suggested by the
above cartoon.

Print answer here

A ⬭⬭⬭⬭ FOR ⬭⬭⬭⬭ ⬭⬭⬭⬭

JUMBLE®

Unscramble these six Jumbles, one letter
to each square, to form six ordinary words.

TEASTE

HERTAG

INPURT

YARMID

THRUNE

EMTYSS

Ugh . . . guess I'll
have to get through
another day

WHAT GETTING
UP EARLY
IN THE MORNING
IS A MATTER OF.

Now arrange the circled letters to form
the surprise answer, as suggested by the
above cartoon.

Print answer here

OVER

JUMBLE®

Unscramble these six Jumbles, one letter to each square, to form six ordinary words.

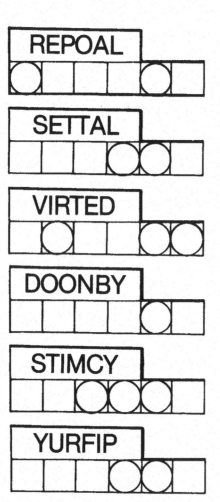

REPOAL

SETTAL

VIRTED

DOONBY

STIMCY

YURFIP

WHAT THAT TOAST GAVE RISE TO.

Now arrange the circled letters to form the surprise answer, as suggested by the above cartoon.

Print answer here

JUMBLE®

Unscramble these six Jumbles, one letter to each square, to form six ordinary words.

CANTIG

UMLOVE

TYNTOK

PHISOL

JOBTEC

DRAISH

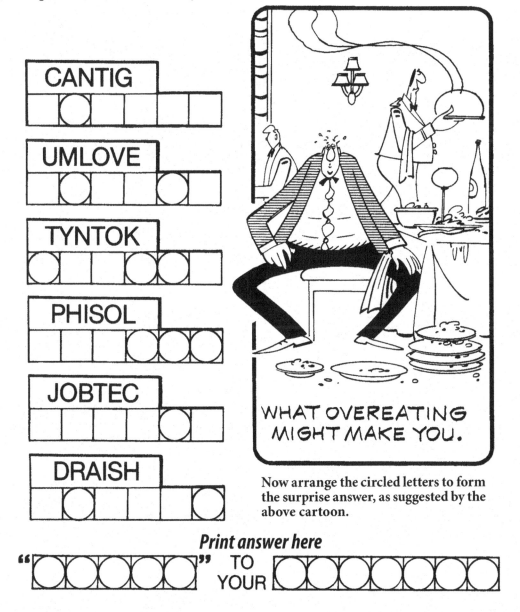

WHAT OVEREATING MIGHT MAKE YOU.

Now arrange the circled letters to form the surprise answer, as suggested by the above cartoon.

Print answer here

" ☐☐☐☐☐ " TO
YOUR ☐☐☐☐☐☐☐

173

JUMBLE®

Unscramble these six Jumbles, one letter to each square, to form six ordinary words.

CALARI

WULTOA

LYROOP

RUHNGY

TUGELL

JUINER

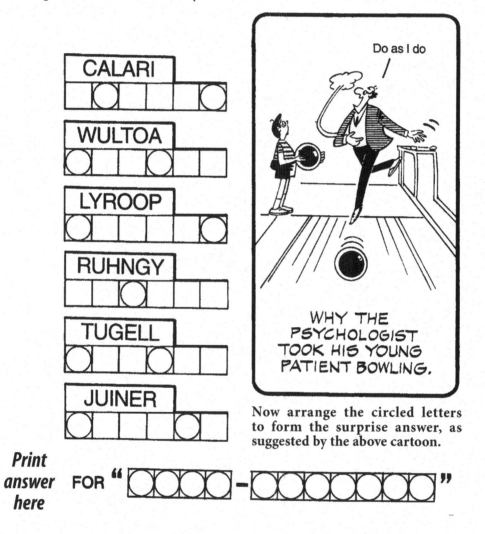

Do as I do

WHY THE PSYCHOLOGIST TOOK HIS YOUNG PATIENT BOWLING.

Now arrange the circled letters to form the surprise answer, as suggested by the above cartoon.

Print answer here

FOR " ⬡⬡⬡⬡ – ⬡⬡⬡⬡⬡⬡⬡ "

174

JUMBLE®

Unscramble these six Jumbles, one letter to each square, to form six ordinary words.

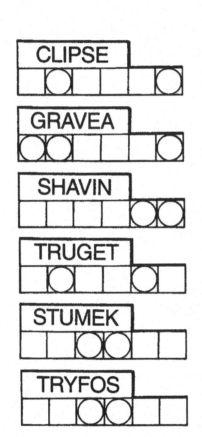

CLIPSE

GRAVEA

SHAVIN

TRUGET

STUMEK

TRYFOS

WHAT CONGRESS CALLED ITS SOUND SYSTEM.

Now arrange the circled letters to form the surprise answer, as suggested by the above cartoon.

Print answer here ⬡⬡⬡⬡⬡⬡⬡⬡ OF THE ⬡⬡⬡⬡⬡

JUMBLE®

Unscramble these six Jumbles, one letter
to each square, to form six ordinary words.

PLINEP

FRIPOT

SEPPIN

TREBUT

CORBON

DEFROC

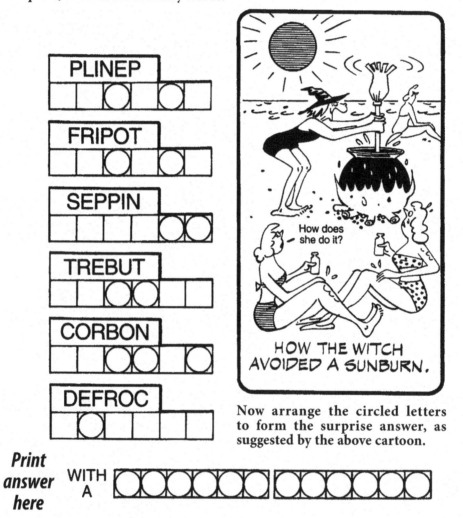

How does
she do it?

HOW THE WITCH
AVOIDED A SUNBURN.

Now arrange the circled letters
to form the surprise answer, as
suggested by the above cartoon.

Print
answer
here

WITH A ⬭⬭⬭⬭⬭⬭ ⬭⬭⬭⬭⬭⬭

JUMBLE®

Unscramble these six Jumbles, one letter to each square, to form six ordinary words.

KORREB

YEMMAH

SAMIPH

SYTHAN

TEXMEP

MOPSIE

Where's the rest of it?

HOW HE DESCRIBED THE SEAFOOD DISH.

Now arrange the circled letters to form the surprise answer, as suggested by the above cartoon.

Print answer here " ⬡⬡⬡⬡⬡ '⬡⬡⬡⬡⬡' "

JUMBLE®

Unscramble these six Jumbles, one letter to each square, to form six ordinary words.

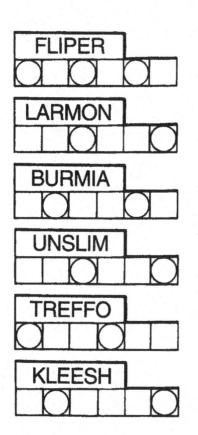

FLIPER

LARMON

BURMIA

UNSLIM

TREFFO

KLEESH

Now for my snappy sales pitch...

WHAT THE SALESMAN USED IN HIS BUSINESS.

Now arrange the circled letters to form the surprise answer, as suggested by the above cartoon.

Print answer here

A "⬭⬭⬭⬭⬭" - ⬭⬭⬭⬭ ⬭⬭⬭⬭⬭

178

JUMBLE

Unscramble these six Jumbles, one letter
to each square, to form six ordinary words.

WHRATT

MYLITE

CIDTUN

GUFNSU

RALEWY

CRECEO

This is the kite they're talking about.

I heard about this.

A CROWD WAS GATHERING
TO SEE THE AMAZING KITE
AFTER PEOPLE ----

Now arrange the circled letters to form
the surprise answer, as suggested by the
above cartoon.

Print answer here

JUMBLE®

Unscramble these six Jumbles, one letter to each square, to form six ordinary words.

TEPCID

ENRUSU

KTERAA

DIDYOT

GARFEO

LANUNA

Now, tell me that doesn't handle better than a minivan. They don't make them like this anymore.

Do you think we're fools?

No, they don't.

Bob's Car-O-Rama

THEY DIDN'T BUY THE CAR AFTER TEST DRIVING IT BECAUSE THEY DIDN'T WANT TO BE ---

Now arrange the circled letters to form the surprise answer, as suggested by the above cartoon.

Print answer here

JUMBLE®

Unscramble these six Jumbles, one letter to each square, to form six ordinary words.

DRACEA

TRUFOH

BRELHA

STCOKE

KREAMT

WUTOIT

I could swear they were up here somewhere.

Where are the crossings?

When can we play?

HE WAS MISSING SOME COMPONENTS FROM HIS MODEL TRAIN SET BECAUSE HE'D ----

Now arrange the circled letters to form the surprise answer, as suggested by the above cartoon.

Print answer here

181

JUMBLE®

Unscramble these six Jumbles, one letter to each square, to form six ordinary words.

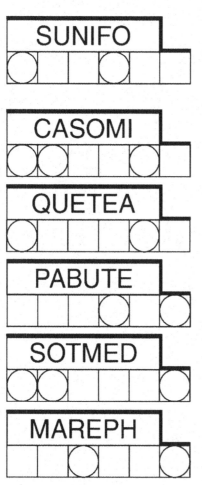

SUNIFO

CASOMI

QUETEA

PABUTE

SOTMED

MAREPH

What happened to the one you bought a few months ago?

You know me. I like to have my watches match my new outfits.

SHE BOUGHT A NEW WRISTWATCH ----

Now arrange the circled letters to form the surprise answer, as suggested by the above cartoon.

Print answer here

182

JUMBLE®

Unscramble these six Jumbles, one letter
to each square, to form six ordinary words.

PARSIN

DEYBOM

YASEFT

ALOHET

RODNAG

USARQE

It's the latest in surgical technology. It even has voice recognition.

Wow! This will streamline our surgeries.

Hello! Shall we begin?

PING

THE SURGERY CENTER'S NEW COMPUTER WAS GOING TO ENHANCE THEIR ---

Now arrange the circled letters to form
the surprise answer, as suggested by the
above cartoon.

Print answer here

183

Answers

1. **Jumbles:** BRIAR FUSSY PARISH GOODLY
   Answer: These athletes can be expected to start prospering—"PROS"

2. **Jumbles:** RAVEN SHEER ADJUST MEASLY
   Answer: What she gave the mountain climber—HER "ASSENT"

3. **Jumbles:** HOARD IDIOT BUSILY FUTILE
   Answer: They're three to one!—THIRDS

4. **Jumbles:** GRIPE TRULY BEGONE FEMALE
   Answer: In case of fire—pull!—THE TRIGGER

5. **Jumbles:** FACET AFTER INCOME CEMENT
   Answer: Comes and goes in the street—TRAFFIC

6. **Jumbles:** NIECE DEITY DRIVEL CHISEL
   Answer: Could be "in the red"—but he's still able to eat out—THE DINER

7. **Jumbles:** VYING GOURD APATHY NESTLE
   Answer: Letters calling for an answer—RSVP

8. **Jumbles:** ETUDE HITCH SUBURB PARADE
   Answer: He might be associated with a crook—A SHEPHERD

9. **Jumbles:** YOUNG TEASE SUBMIT AMAZON
   Answer: "No charge unless it's fixed"—A BAYONET

10. **Jumbles:** KNIFE BURST DAHLIA ATOMIC
    Answer: Four-fifths of it is wooden but it still tastes good—"S-TEAK"

11. **Jumbles:** LADLE FAIRY TEMPER CARBON
    Answer: Sounds as though the criminal was not a woman—THE "MALE-FACTOR"

12. **Jumbles:** GNARL EATEN STOLEN PROFIT
    Answer: They don't have to be civil when they do their work—ENGINEERS

13. **Jumbles:** NAVAL MINER WALLOP DEMISE
    Answer: Such a man is really of low degree—A SNOWMAN

14. **Jumbles:** CHEEK HAVOC SCHOOL AIRWAY
    Answer: Evidently this kind of owl doesn't give a hoot!—A SCREECH OWL

15. **Jumbles:** BAGGY JOLLY FOIBLE VARIED
    Answer: The shape of things to come in the poultry business—OVAL

16. **Jumbles:** PIKER TEMPO SEXTON BURIAL
    Answer: Their efforts bring credit to their country—EXPORTERS

17. **Jumbles:** HEDGE COACH DISCUS GRISLY
    Answer: Designed to support the members at the bottom—SHOES

18. **Jumbles:** HOARY ABBOT NEPHEW HONEST
    Answer: You can draw this as long as you live—BREATH

19. **Jumbles:** LEAVE WOVEN DECENT AFLOAT
    Answer: Nothing paid yet—and no objections!—"ALL-OWED"

20. **Jumbles:** FENCE ALIAS EMBALM GUZZLE
    Answer: A sign that one's reducing—MINUS

21. **Jumbles:** KHAKI SANDY SALUTE FIGURE
    Answer: When blue things might look brighter—THE SKY

22. **Jumbles:** GULCH JEWEL ANGINA HOMING
    Answer: That "Bull" across the Atlantic—"JOHN"

23. **Jumbles:** OZONE GROUP INVEST GAITER
    Answer: What organs might also produce—GROANS

24. **Jumbles:** LEECH AMUSE SIMILE TREATY
    Answer: Goes into liquidation when the heat's on—MELTS

25. **Jumbles:** INEPT BATON INFUSE BABIED
    Answer: Sounds crazy about baseball—"BATS"

26. **Jumbles:** DADDY SNARL MINGLE QUARTZ
    Answer: First person possessive—ADAM'S

27. **Jumbles:** PANDA UNITY BRUTAL CORNEA
    Answer: The most famous heart specialist—CUPID

28. **Jumbles:** LIBEL CURRY JUSTLY MUCOUS
    Answer: Sufferers from this agree it could be cruel—ULCER

29. **Jumbles:** HOVEL FAMED SIZZLE NEGATE
    Answer: His sole companion—A HEEL

30. **Jumbles:** CATCH SCOUR OUTING PERMIT
    Answer: "I get out of Spain—going across a river!"—"SPAN"

31. **Jumbles:** PYLON SWOON MELODY GRUBBY
    Answer: In a word, it means the same thing!—SYNONYM

32. **Jumbles:** COVEY NOOSE TRUANT GLUTEN
    Answer: Might provide backing for a play—SCENERY

33. **Jumbles:** PUPIL CUBIC BESTOW SHOULD
    Answer: The caveman's strongest suit—CLUBS

34. **Jumbles:** ARMOR SPITE GOATEE HANDED
    Answer: Rub away!—"ERASE"

35. **Jumbles:** LIMBO CEASE SAVORY AWEIGH
    Answer: Feels sick—from a sail—AILS

36. **Jumbles:** WAGER BYLAW COMPEL SOOTHE
    Answer: What a life on the ocean wave is—"SWELL"

37. **Jumbles:** NATAL BROIL CARPET ZODIAC
    Answer: A former leading lady in Russia—CZARINA

38. **Jumbles:** CHIDE USURY EXCISE NORMAL
    Answer: May be taken from home with pleasure—AN EXCURSION

39. **Jumbles:** ROBIN DECAY ENCORE STANZA
    Answer: A notable increase—CRESCENDO

40. **Jumbles:** WEDGE HOBBY LAYOFF SURELY
    Answer: This liquid might be deceiving—EYEWASH

41. **Jumbles:** LEAKY CREEL GENDER FORGET
    Answer: What you might find in the gallery—"ALLERGY"

42. **Jumbles:** BIRCH LOVER FLABBY GADFLY
    Answer: Ask a burning question—GRILL

43. **Jumbles:** DRONE FUDGE INFECT TWINGE
    Answer: What you wouldn't have a single reason for getting—A WEDDING GIFT

44. **Jumbles:** ESSAY TABOO FINITE MENACE
    Answer: Where logs aren't for burning—AT SEA

45. **Jumbles:** TYING SCARY DURESS FESTAL
    Answer: Remains—to provide support—STAYS

46. **Jumbles:** COLON VIPER FIXING IMPUTE
    Answer: Makes you feel put out—EVICTION

47. **Jumbles:** LOGIC BLAZE VICUNA CANNED
    Answer: What the Stone Age man did when he came home late one night—CAVED IN

48. **Jumbles:** MILKY ALTAR COMEDY SYLVAN
    Answer: What that awful singer was—A "VOCAL-AMITY"

49. **Jumbles:** BATHE ENACT KOSHER ARCADE
    Answer: What a tasteful necktie should be—SEEN BUT NOT "HEARD"

50. **Jumbles:** CHICK TAFFY ARCTIC BRUTAL
    Answer: What dermatology is the science of—"ITCH CRAFT"

51. **Jumbles:** PRUNE DRONE KISMET ARTFUL
    Answer: What a flatterer seldom is—INTERRUPTED

52. **Jumbles:** LIBEL ALIVE SAVORY CLOUDY
    Answer: How that comical sergeant started the day for his troops—WITH "DROLL" CALL

53. **Jumbles:** COUGH FUROR MULISH APATHY
Answer: What the acrobat made a success of—A "FLOP"

54. **Jumbles:** BASIS PEACE NUTRIA AMOEBA
Answer: What the poorest waiters in some restaurants are—CUSTOMERS

55. **Jumbles:** NOISE LOUSY AMBUSH SHOULD
Answer: Was the clam digger this?—"MUSSEL" BOUND

56. **Jumbles:** BROOK HAREM STODGY APIECE
Answer: Full of beans!—A POD

57. **Jumbles:** MUSIC ABATE SONATA EMPLOY
Answer: What she thought her husband's credit card was—A "BUY" PASS

58. **Jumbles:** CHIDE OWING ASSAIL INFANT
Answer: People go to great "lengths" to reduce this—WIDTHS

59. **Jumbles:** DAILY BUXOM SOIREE BONNET
Answer: What people with tireless energy often become—TIRESOME

60. **Jumbles:** UNCLE ALBUM BEHIND OUTFIT
Answer: What that gorgeous sky was—"BLUE-TIFUL"

61. **Jumbles:** STUNG HUSKY BUNION DAINTY
Answer: When the famous star didn't show up, his stand-in became this—A STANDOUT

62. **Jumbles:** EMERY STEED MILDEW PURITY
Answer: What a belly dancer has to know how to do—TWIDDLE HER "TUM"

63. **Jumbles:** DECRY JEWEL GAINED LUNACY
Answer: That hammy magician knew how to make this disappear—THE AUDIENCE

64. **Jumbles:** ELEGY PRIZE VASSAL FOURTH
Answer: When you invite someone to an outrageously expensive restaurant—IT SERVES YOU RIGHT

65. **Jumbles:** BIPED MOTIF GOODLY FRUGAL
Answer: The insomniac was advised to sleep on the edge of his bed in order to do this without delay—"DROP OFF"

66. **Jumbles:** NOVEL FINIS ABSURD POLISH
Answer: What the guy who just pretended he was a gangster must have been—A "FALSE HOOD"

67. **Jumbles:** NERVY SWISH RITUAL STICKY
Answer: What some decided to do when trousers first became fashionable for women—SKIRT THE ISSUE

68. **Jumbles:** RAVEN PRIOR HUMBLE DEPICT
Answer: The barber told him stories that could do this—CURL HIS HAIR

69. **Jumbles:** JERKY PUDGY WALNUT NINETY
Answer: What the sleazy restaurant that made those awful submarine sandwiches did—WENT UNDER

70. **Jumbles:** MINCE UNCAP SMOKER IMPOSE
Answer: When they wanted to find out about the big bicycle merger, they interviewed this—THE "SPOKES-MAN"

71. **Jumbles:** IVORY TOXIN HECKLE SALUTE
Answer: Why the judge couldn't be disturbed at dinner—HIS HONOR WAS AT "STEAK"

72. **Jumbles:** OXIDE PROBE ENGINE DAMAGE
Answer: What the maestro called his assistant—HIS "BAND AIDE"

73. **Jumbles:** LILAC HASTY TRICKY STYMIE
Answer: What they agreed to when they organized the card game on the plane—THE SKY'S THE LIMIT

74. **Jumbles:** IMBUE BUSHY MORTAR GULLET
Answer: Another name for a pirate ship—A "THUG" BOAT

75. **Jumbles:** IRONY EXPEL PLOWED GUILTY
Answer: What happened when the price of duck feathers increased—DOWN WENT UP

76. **Jumbles:** FETCH LISLE WALLOP NATURE
Answer: What that prize-winning dog was—A SHOW "ARF"

77. **Jumbles:** TITLE DITTY LIZARD TEAPOT
Answer: What the gossipy rattlesnake was—A TATTLE "TAIL"

78. **Jumbles:** POWER CRAWL LAVISH NICETY
Answer: What they called those motorized nuts—"CYCLE-PATHS"

79. **Jumbles:** HONOR DUCAL COUSIN BALLAD
Answer: When he became top banana he lost touch with this—THE OLD BUNCH

80. **Jumbles:** HOVEL MOTIF AGENDA ELIXIR
Answer: A jury never works right when it's this—"FIXED"

81. **Jumbles:** HARPY SUITE BESIDE RECTOR
Answer: What some people's. handwriting is—A "SCRIPT" TEASE

82. **Jumbles:** BYLAW MADLY CHERUB FLORAL
Answer: What they thought it was when the wimp tried to act like a wolf—A "HOWL"

83. **Jumbles:** PHONY SCOUT MUFFLE GULLET
Answer: Where's the fencing master?—OUT TO "LUNGE"

84. **Jumbles:** WHINE SYLPH JUSTLY QUARRY
Answer: What the stand-up comedian equips himself with—QUIPS

85. **Jumbles:** TESTY RAJAH HALLOW SPEEDY
Answer: Could this be another name for that health club?—THE "SWEAT SHOP"

86. **Jumbles:** YOKEL KHAKI ENMITY CONVEX
Answer: The only voice that dad sometimes has in family affairs—"INVOICE"

87. **Jumbles:** BURST LIMIT MOSAIC TOFFEE
Answer: What Dracula got when he mistook a snowman for a human being—FROSTBITE

88. **Jumbles:** BRAVO DITTY INTENT TURTLE
Answer: What to pay if you don't want to spend too much—ATTENTION

89. **Jumbles:** FILMY QUEST MURMUR BUSHEL
Answer: He deserves to do this when he behaves like a worm—SQUIRM

90. **Jumbles:** YEARN LINER QUAINT TYPING
Answer: What the dishonest inventor obviously was—A PATENT LIAR

91. **Jumbles:** NOTCH OUNCE UPKEEP COOKIE
Answer: What the poultry farmer called the car he drove to market—HIS CHICKEN COUPE

92. **Jumbles:** ACUTE BAKED FORBID UNSEAT
Answer: What the tired manager of the quaint inn looked forward to—BED AND BREAKFAST

93. **Jumbles:** VERVE VITAL HECTIC TARGET
Answer: Why magnets are found on refrigerators—THEY'RE ATTRACTIVE

94. **Jumbles:** GLADE QUEER GIMLET FOIBLE
Answer: What the thief got at the computer store—A MEGA BITE

95. **Jumbles:** RHYME PANDA GOITER WIDEST
Answer: The kind of conversation found in a bar—SPIRITED

96. **Jumbles:** DALLY BROOD TEMPER WOEFUL
Answer: What the art thief said he was—FRAMED

97. **Jumbles:** SOGGY OXIDE EMBODY FABLED
Answer: What the successful realtor was known for—HIS GOOD "DEEDS"

98. **Jumbles:** BRIAR AORTA TINGLE FORAGE
Answer: What kind of relationship the twins had in college—FRATERNAL

185

99. **Jumbles:** FORGO FIFTY WINNOW MINGLE
Answer: Why the watchmaker didn't get the raise—
HIS TIMING WAS OFF

100. **Jumbles:** LEAFY NIECE STYLUS MUSTER
Answer: What new actors become a part of—THE CAST SYSTEM

101. **Jumbles:** THUMB KAYAK SPRING EXPAND
Answer: The hula dancer was really sick. She had a bad cold and
she couldn't—SHAKE IT

102. **Jumbles:** SHYLY GLORY NIMBLE NOODLE
Answer: They bought the house next to the horse farm because
they loved the—"NEIGH-BORS"

103. **Jumbles:** IMAGE DROOP ORNERY LAWFUL
Answer: The frog couldn't build a deck where he lived, but he
was able to make a—"PADIO"

104. **Jumbles:** SIXTY SENSE PILEUP TYRANT
Answer: His ability to brew such amazing Earl Grey, chamomile
and chai was a result of his—"EXPERT-TEAS"

105. **Jumbles:** FOAMY SWISH FONDUE DIVERT
Answer: Afer a competing lemonade seller moved in next to
her, she was—STANDOFFISH

106. **Jumbles:** TARDY NIECE WEAKEN TATTOO
Answer: When the cartoonist sketched the White House guard
he—DREW ATTENTION

107. **Jumbles:** RIGOR GLADE DRAGON CLOSET
Answer: The barbecue on the Army base was led by the—
"GRILL" SERGEANT

108. **Jumbles:** RISKY AMUSE CASINO OUTLET
Answer: After the stationery store closed for the evening,
everything was—STATIONARY

109. **Jumbles:** TEMPT RODEO FOURTH CRUMMY
Answer: The mechanic who loved to talk about engines was a—
MOTOR MOUTH

110. **Jumbles:** ABIDE TWIRL URCHIN LESSON
Answer: The hot dog was OK, but he really wished he could
have—RELISHED IT

111. **Jumbles:** DWELL HANDY ENZYME AWAKEN
Answer: She needed new tires for her car, and the tire salesman
was ready to—WHEEL AND DEAL

112. **Jumbles:** IGLOO AUDIO MEMBER NICELY
Answer: After they struck gold, the owner of the gold mine was
a—"BULLION-AIRE"

113. **Jumbles:** BLOCK PRONE BEACON IRONIC
Answer: When it came to answering questions about his new
novel, the author was an—OPEN BOOK

114. **Jumbles:** AWFUL IMAGE FLAUNT INDIGO
Answer: His heirs all wanted a piece of his fortune, but he was—
UNWILLING

115. **Jumbles:** DRILL PLUCK SUMMER MUTATE
Answer: The tug-of-war was going well until he—
PULLED A MUSCLE

116. **Jumbles:** DOOZY ROYAL WINDOW SUBMIT
Answer: He told Casper the ghost his secret because he knew
Casper—WOULDN'T SAY BOO

117. **Jumbles:** APRON LIMIT IMMUNE MYSELF
Answer: Installation of the new clock was completed in a—
TIMELY MANNER

118. **Jumbles:** ALPHA TWIRL LOCKET LAVISH
Answer: The shopper demanded 50% off everything in the store
because she wanted to—"HALVE" IT ALL

119. **Jumbles:** MOUND SNIFF GALLEY SWAMPY
Answer: The waterfowl's final performance was her—
SWAN SONG

120. **Jumbles:** HEFTY KHAKI WALRUS KITTEN
Answer: He said the painting of the Mongolian leader was a
Picasso, but it was made by a—"KHAN" ARTIST

121. **Jumbles:** STUNT SENSE NOODLE LOCALE
Answer: When it came to places to build a home, the new
subdivision had—LOTS AND LOTS

122. **Jumbles:** PLANT USHER FORBID ELIXIR
Answer: The spaceship's orbit encircling the planet was a—
ROUND TRIP

123. **Jumbles:** EXERT AGAIN SEASON SALMON
Answer: The bull would lose the arm-wrestling match because
he wasn't—STRONG AS AN OX

124. **Jumbles:** FORCE OMEGA UNKIND VACANT
Answer: To transport his cows, the farmer rented a—
"MOO-VING" TRUCK

125. **Jumbles:** AVOID OCTET FORBID OBLONG
Answer: Sasquatch was easy to track because he had a—
BIG FOOT

126. **Jumbles:** FRONT CEASE AWHILE SPIRAL
Answer: To become a rodeo star, the teenager would need to—
LEARN THE ROPES

127. **Jumbles:** CHOMP TALLY LOADED CHANCE
Answer: When King Arthur went to the desert, he visited the—
CAMEL LOT

128. **Jumbles:** FORUM FLASH DISOWN TATTOO
Answer: When they cranked up the music while doing laundry,
they had—LOADS OF FUN

129. **Jumbles:** BEIGE APRON CACKLE CHARGE
Answer: John Lennon wasn't certain he'd like the pizza, but he
decided to give the—"PIECE" A CHANCE

130. **Jumbles:** WIPER DOUBT WISDOM TANGLE
Answer: The drinks at the undersea bar were—WATERED DOWN

131. **Jumbles:** MIMIC MONEY MANAGE WEASEL
Answer: When they taught their puppies how to dog paddle,
things went—SWIMMINGLY

132. **Jumbles:** MODEM BURRO CRANNY FEMALE
Answer: The attendant was well-liked and efficient. They loved
his—ORDERLY MANNER

133. **Jumbles:** TRACK SHOWN POETIC FAMOUS
Answer: When George Reeves got the role of Clark Kent on TV,
he said—THAT'S SUPER, MAN

134. **Jumbles:** CROAK YUCKY BROKEN UPDATE
Answer: He asked if he could join their poker game, and they
said—YOU BET YOU CAN

135. **Jumbles:** MOUND POISE MODULE WRITER
Answer: They sold and sampled a wide variety of wines.
Customers loved the—"EM-POUR-IUM"

136. **Jumbles:** BRING LOGIC SUFFIX GENIUS
Answer: When the aliens landed on the highway, they saw—
SIGNS OF LIFE

137. **Jumbles:** WRECK BEIGE HEAVEN WRENCH
Answer: He was 100 pounds heavier—"WEIGH" BACK WHEN

138. **Jumbles:** VOUCH ELECT LOOSEN SEASON
Answer: When the deck builder told them he did high-quality
work, he wasn't being—ON THE LEVEL

139. **Jumbles:** INEPT MERCY AUTHOR CATCHY
Answer: They found ice on the moon and were attempting to—
UNEARTH IT

140. **Jumbles:** BRISK FANCY EASILY TUGGED
Answer: After weighting herself, and seeing she'd lost 50
pounds, she had a—BIG FAT GRIN

141. **Jumbles:** IGLOO STOMP CAUGHT WOBBLE
Answer: Now that the exterminator's home was overrun with
the ghosts of insects, it had—BUGABOOS

186

142. **Jumbles:** HOUSE BINGO MAYHEM DRIVER
Answer: He replaced his horse's shoes because it—
BEHOOVED HIM

143. **Jumbles:** MOLDY FLUID WALRUS JACKET
Answer: He slowed down for the people on the horses because they had the—"RIDE" OF WAY

144. **Jumbles:** FILMY FIFTY BECKON VORTEX
Answer: The warehouse equipment operator began his midday meal with a—FORK LIFT

145. **Jumbles:** LIMIT HOBBY UNEVEN STOOGE
Answer: The greenskeeper was upset when a gopher made a—HOLE IN ONE

146. **Jumbles:** BLURT LEAKY EMBLEM INWARD
Answer: When it came to whether worms or lures attract more fish, it was—"DE-BAIT-ABLE"

147. **Jumbles:** DRESS UNDUE SPRAIN NEGATE
Answer: When Andrew Johnson was impeached on Feb. 24, 1868, it was—"UN-PRESIDENT-ED"

148. **Jumbles:** BOOTH DIZZY CALMLY BLEACH
Answer: The panda wanted to buy the world's fastest growing plant, but he was being—BAMBOOZLED

149. **Jumbles:** DINKY DOOZY SHAKEN LAGOON
Answer: When it came to learning sign language, the student was—IN GOOD HANDS

150. **Jumbles:** BIRCH PUTTY CHROME EXEMPT
Answer: When the town needed to make big purchases, it had to be handled—"BUY" COMMITTEE

151. **Jumbles:** DOUSE BURST SMOOTH FONDUE
Answer: Trying to plant flowers in the rocky soil was—NO BED OF ROSES

152. **Jumbles:** CLOTH ABIDE ABSURD FORGET
Answer: The reptiles had problems commuting in the Everglades because of the—"TAIL-GATORS"

153. **Jumbles:** ONION UPPER NUGGET ACCRUE
Answer: Before her upcoming speech to the legislature, the senator did much—"PREP-ORATION"

154. **Jumbles:** GROUP BROWN SOCIAL WICKET
Answer: The former NFL QB rolled seven strikes in a row. People gathered to watch his—SUPER BOWLING

155. **Jumbles:** CHECK TANGY SUMMON PEWTER
Answer: The cosmetology student missed her exam and needed to take a—MAKEUP TEST

156. **Jumbles:** TAKEN FUSSY DIVEST COTTON
Answer: They were hoping to get a discount on a granite countertop, but the price was—SET IN STONE

157. **Jumbles:** IMAGE TOKEN TRENCH COUPON
Answer: It was easy to spot the king and queen of the school dance, because they were—PROMINENT

158. **Jumbles:** HANDY WEAVE REBUKE CHOSEN
Answer: When the beer makers argued over who made better beer, the result was a—"BREW-HAHA"

159. **Jumbles:** WHEAT COUNT SHADOW WEIGHT
Answer: The identical twin boys dressed so differently because—"TWO" EACH HIS OWN

160. **Jumbles:** PETTY KIOSK HUMANE CIRCUS
Answer: He wouldn't stop complaining about the wine, so his wife wanted him to—PUT A CORK IN IT

161. **Jumbles:** FIESTA TONGUE BEFORE STYMIE CATCHY POLITE
Answer: You might have a vested interest in this—A THREE-PIECE SUIT

162. **Jumbles:** WHENCE BELONG MODISH SUBDUE FOSSIL LOUNGE
Answer: What a good body snatcher wouldn't be without on a night like this—HIS "GHOUL-OSHES"

163. **Jumbles:** WATERY BAFFLE CRAYON VOYAGE TANDEM ENSIGN
Answer: What you wouldn't expect to get from a man of few words—A LONG SENTENCE

164. **Jumbles:** NIMBLE UNLOAD BUTTON ENABLE KILLER CHOSEN
Answer: What the talkative whale was—A BIG BLUBBERMOUTH

165. **Jumbles:** ENJOIN HOPPER DISARM BLOUSE ZIGZAG ENTITY
Answer: At a place like this expect them at closing time—PARTING SHOTS

166. **Jumbles:** PARITY FLUNKY NORMAL INVOKE ENCORE FROTHY
Answer: What would you say if the sea dried up?—"WE HAVEN'T A NOTION"

167. **Jumbles:** LEVITY MASCOT DRAGON MODEST HEARSE PACKET
Answer: What an opththalmologist's office is—A SITE FOR SORE EYES

168. **Jumbles:** ESTATE GATHER TURNIP MYRIAD HUNTER SYSTEM
Answer: What getting up early in the morning is a matter of—MIND OVER MATTRESS

169. **Jumbles:** PAROLE LATEST DIVERT NOBODY MYSTIC PURIFY
Answer: What that toast gave rise to—LIFTED SPIRITS

170. **Jumbles:** ACTING VOLUME KNOTTY POLISH OBJECT RADISH
Answer: What overeating might make you—"THICK" TO YOUR STOMACH

171. **Jumbles:** RACIAL OUTLAW POORLY HUNGRY GULLET INJURE
Answer: Why the psychologist took his young patient bowling—FOR "ROLL-PLAYING"

172. **Jumbles:** SPLICE RAVAGE VANISH GUTTER MUSKET FROSTY
Answer: What Congress called its sound system—SPEAKERS OF THE HOUSE

173. **Jumbles:** NIPPLE PROFIT PEPSIN BUTTER BRONCO FORCED
Answer: How the witch avoided a sunburn—WITH A LOTION POTION

174. **Jumbles:** BROKEN MAYHEM MISHAP SHANTY EXEMPT IMPOSE
Answer: How he described the seafood dish—"SHRIMP 'SKIMPY'"

175. **Jumbles:** PILFER NORMAL BARIUM MUSLIN EFFORT SHEKEL
Answer: What the salesman used in his business—A "SELL"-ULAR PHONE

176. **Jumbles:** THWART TIMELY INDUCT FUNGUS LAWYER COERCE
Answer: A crowd was gathering to see the amazing kite after people—CAUGHT WIND OF IT

177. **Jumbles:** DEPICT UNSURE KARATE ODDITY FORAGE ANNUAL
Answer: They didn't buy the car after test driving it because they didn't want to be—TAKEN FOR A RIDE

178. **Jumbles:** ARCADE FOURTH HERBAL SOCKET MARKET OUTWIT
Answer: He was missing some components from his model train set because he'd—LOST TRACK OF THEM

179. **Jumbles:** FUSION MOSAIC EQUATE UPBEAT MODEST HAMPER
Answer: She bought a new wristwatch—FROM TIME TO TIME

180. **Jumbles:** SPRAIN EMBODY SAFETY LOATHE DRAGON SQUARE
Answer: The surgery center's new computer was going to enhance their—OPERATING SYSTEM

Need More Jumbles®?

Order any of these books through your bookseller or call Triumph Books toll-free at 800-888-4741.

Jumble® Books

More than 175 puzzles each!

Cowboy Jumble®
· ISBN: 978-1-62937-355-3

Jammin' Jumble®
· ISBN: 978-1-57243-844-6

Java Jumble®
· ISBN: 978-1-60078-415-6

Jet Set Jumble®
· ISBN: 978-1-60078-353-1

Jolly Jumble®
· ISBN: 978-1-60078-214-5

Jumble® Anniversary
· ISBN: 987-1-62937-734-6

Jumble® Ballet
· ISBN: 978-1-62937-616-5

Jumble® Birthday
· ISBN: 978-1-62937-652-3

Jumble® Celebration
· ISBN: 978-1-60078-134-6

Jumble® Champion
· ISBN: 978-1-62937-870-1

Jumble® Coronation
· ISBN: 978-1-62937-976-0

Jumble® Cuisine
· ISBN: 978-1-62937-735-3

Jumble® Drag Race
· ISBN: 978-1-62937-483-3

Jumble® Ever After
· ISBN: 978-1-62937-785-8

Jumble® Explorer
· ISBN: 978-1-60078-854-3

Jumble® Explosion
· ISBN: 978-1-60078-078-3

Jumble® Fever
· ISBN: 978-1-57243-593-3

Jumble® Galaxy
· ISBN: 978-1-60078-583-2

Jumble® Garden
· ISBN: 978-1-62937-653-0

Jumble® Genius
· ISBN: 978-1-57243-896-5

Jumble® Geography
· ISBN: 978-1-62937-615-8

Jumble® Getaway
· ISBN: 978-1-60078-547-4

Jumble® Gold
· ISBN: 978-1-62937-354-6

Jumble® Health
· ISBN: 978-1-63727-085-1

Jumble® Jackpot
· ISBN: 978-1-57243-897-2

Jumble® Jailbreak
· ISBN: 978-1-62937-002-6

Jumble® Jambalaya
· ISBN: 978-1-60078-294-7

Jumble® Jitterbug
· ISBN: 978-1-60078-584-9

Jumble® Journey
· ISBN: 978-1-62937-549-6

Jumble® Jubilation
· ISBN: 978-1-62937-784-1

Jumble® Jubilee
· ISBN: 978-1-57243-231-4

Jumble® Juggernaut
· ISBN: 978-1-60078-026-4

Jumble® Kingdom
· ISBN: 978-1-62937-079-8

Jumble® Knockout
· ISBN: 978-1-62937-078-1

Jumble® Madness
· ISBN: 978-1-892049-24-7

Jumble® Magic
· ISBN: 978-1-60078-795-9

Jumble® Mania
· ISBN: 978-1-57243-697-8

Jumble® Marathon
· ISBN: 978-1-60078-944-1

Jumble® Masterpiece
· ISBN: 978-1-62937-916-6

Jumble® Neighbor
· ISBN: 978-1-62937-845-9

Jumble® Parachute
· ISBN: 978-1-62937-548-9

Jumble® Party
· ISBN: 978-1-63727-008-0

Jumble® Safari
· ISBN: 978-1-60078-675-4

Jumble® Sensation
· ISBN: 978-1-60078-548-1

Jumble® Skyscraper
· ISBN: 978-1-62937-869-5

Jumble® Symphony
· ISBN: 978-1-62937-131-3

Jumble® Theater
· ISBN: 978-1-62937-484-0

Jumble® Time Machine: 1972
· ISBN: 978-1-63727-082-0

Jumble® Trouble
· ISBN: 978-1-62937-917-3

Jumble® University
· ISBN: 978-1-62937-001-9

Jumble® Unleashed
· ISBN: 978-1-62937-844-2

Jumble® Vacation
· ISBN: 978-1-60078-796-6

Jumble® Wedding
· ISBN: 978-1-62937-307-2

Jumble® Workout
· ISBN: 978-1-60078-943-4

Jump, Jive and Jumble®
· ISBN: 978-1-60078-215-2

Lunar Jumble®
· ISBN: 978-1-60078-853-6

Monster Jumble®
· ISBN: 978-1-62937-213-6

Mystic Jumble®
· ISBN: 978-1-62937-130-6

Rainy Day Jumble®
· ISBN: 978-1-60078-352-4

Royal Jumble®
· ISBN: 978-1-60078-738-6

Sports Jumble®
· ISBN: 978-1-57243-113-3

Summer Fun Jumble®
· ISBN: 978-1-57243-114-0

Touchdown Jumble®
· ISBN: 978-1-62937-212-9

Oversize Jumble® Books

More than 500 puzzles!

Colossal Jumble®
· ISBN: 978-1-57243-490-5

Jumbo Jumble®
· ISBN: 978-1-57243-314-4

Jumble® Crosswords™

More than 175 puzzles!

Jumble® Crosswords™
· ISBN: 978-1-57243-347-2